PRAISE FOR BOOKS BY

M000120317

SIDE BY SIDE

"Susan Tiberghien's multi-layered reflections inspired by nature and grounded in daily life speak to couples at all stages of growth. For those setting off on the eternal journey into the labyrinth of love and marriage, there can be no better guide."

— Patti M. Marxsen, author of *Helene Schweitzer: A Life of Her Own*

"What a unique gift Susan Tiberghien has given the reader: an invitation to journal about the one you love and to share it with him or her, reliving and rekindling the experience of your relationship. Reading about her ongoing courtship with her husband of over 50 years, *Side by Side* reminds us about what is possible in a long sustaining love and encourages us to write about our own love story. In language both sensuous and lyrical, Tiberghien reminds us of who we were when the first blush of love opened our hearts to the world."

— Maureen Murdock, author of *Unreliable Truth: On Memoir and Memory*

LOOKING FOR GOLD

"*Looking for Gold* is a laboratory for artists, dreamers, and all who seek for ways to realize their true gold."

— Robert Bosnak, author of *The Little Course in Dreams*

CIRCLING TO THE CENTER

"A gracefully written memoir of her own responses to grace, *Circling to the Center* is the result of being called to deeper prayer life, tapping the source within, resting in unknowing and opening up to newness and rebirth.... Like Thomas Merton, Tiberghien draws upon her own experience to lead the reader from the circumference of unique circumstances to the common center, 'our one same center—our one same source [for] all the circles are concentric.'"

— Barbara Cliff Stoodley, author of *The Merton Seasonal*

FOOTSTEPS

"Stitched together from essays, poems, photographs and even family recipes, Susan Tiberghien's elegant memoir combines all the intimacy of a family album with the wisdom of her vivid prose and poetry.... The journey ends at the place it started—the contemplative self—and in the silence of her youngest son's empty room, where she writes, 'I sit at my old oak desk, the drawers now filled with stories... I close my eyes and look within.'"

— Elaine Vitone, contributor to *Creative Nonfiction*

"Footsteps: In Love with a Frenchman is a charming, heartfelt journey into European culture and cuisine, the beauty and loneliness of unfamiliar places, and the exquisite good fortune of finding a lifelong companion. Tiberghien's essays are a rich bouillabaisse of scenic detail and delicious memories. Just a lovely book."

— Dinty W. Moore, author of *Dear Mister Essay Writer Guy*

ONE YEAR TO A WRITING LIFE

"One Year to a Writing Life is beautifully pitched and covers a very broad terrain very sensibly and sensitively.... Tiberghien produces so many and various examples that many different tastes and artistic leanings can be satisfied and nothing germane is ever sacrificed. I consider this book, in its quiet and dedicated way, a model of what a clear-sighted, encouraging, helpful primer should be, and I'll certainly be recommending it to students."

— Michael Hulse, author of *The 20th Century in Poetry*, co-editor

"Susan Tiberghien is an artist of the word, the thought, the soul."

— M.M. Tawfik, author of *A Naughty Boy Called Antar*

Side *by* Side

WRITING YOUR LOVE STORY

SUSAN M. TIBERGHIEN

Side *by* Side

WRITING YOUR LOVE STORY

Red Lotus Studio Press

Red Lotus Studio Press
New York, New York
Facebook.com/RedLotusStudioPress
info@theredlotusreview.com

Publisher: Melissa A. Rosati
Editor: Betsy Robinson
Cover, text design and typography by Infinitum Limited.
Printed by CreateSpace, a DBA of On-Demand Publishing, LLC
This book is available for wholesale and retail distribution through
Amazon Extended Distribution.

Red Lotus Studio Press books are available at special discounts for
bulk purchases in the United States by corporations, institutions,
and other organizations. For more information, please contact
info@theredlotusreview.com

Published in the United States by Red Lotus Studio Press, a DBA of
Melissa's Coaching Studio, LLC.

ISBN 978-0-9961660-1-0 (paper)—978-0-9961660-3-4 (ebook)

Photography credits are listed at the end of the text.

CONTENTS

JOURNAL PRACTICES

Introduction

PIERRE AND I HAVE BEEN MARRIED FOR FIFTY-FIVE YEARS, and we are still very much in love. What went right? To answer this question, I thought back to the good moments of our relationship and began to write. With each memory, I relived the experience—the strong attraction that has kept us together for so long. When I shared the memories with Pierre, we felt the attraction together.

This is the premise of *Side by Side*: that we can think back to some of the good moments of our relationships; write about them, living them anew, seeing the colors, listening to the sounds, feeling the emotions; and that we each can then share memories with our partner, awakening the mutual desire to create new good moments. I suggest that we can write our way to lasting love. And we can do so side by side with our spouse or partner, while respecting the space between us—filling each other's cup, as Kahlil Gibran writes in *The Prophet*, but drinking not from the same cup.

I write about my own love story as an example and an invitation. It is the story of a long marriage, a long relationship. I speak of marriage and relationship interchangeably, as I speak of spouse and partner. Pierre is both. He is my lover, the father of my children, and my best friend.

I trace the story of our marriage in seven ongoing and overlapping steps, seven chapters, starting with courtship and commitment, two components which I see as central to lasting love. The story expands by looking both outward and inward, while we continue to grow. And ends with wellbeing and celebration, everyday celebrations of our togetherness.

Each chapter is introduced with a recent journal entry to open the door and usher you into the practice of writing. I wrote these entries a year ago during a week in the fall, as examples of everyday journaling. They open the door to the memories that follow, memories of courtship to memories of celebration, from the early years of our marriage up to the present, to the Indian summer that Pierre and I are now living.

Interspersed in the pages of my memories are pages for your memories, with suggestions for writing your own journal entries. These pages, titled Journal Practices, invite you to write a memory of a personal experience that you shared with your partner. There are questions and prompts as well as counsel from several of my favorite writers and teachers—Rainer Maria Rilke, Brenda Ueland, William Zinsser, Dorothea Brande, Annie Dillard, and Thomas Merton. Each journal practice asks you to write for ten minutes, just a few paragraphs. To sit down with pen and paper and let your hand lead you into the experience, into the memory.

The word "journal" comes from the French word *jour*, day. The root is also found in the word "journey." Journal writing is a journey. A journey in self-discovery. When you sit down to write, something begins to flow. It's like walking. With each step, you walk further. With each journal entry, you write further. I have kept a journal for years, turning to it to find my way—as spouse, mother, writer, teacher—through writing. I no longer write in it every day. But I always have it with me. I'll write about something that happened, that I observed, that I read. A dream, a reflection, a conversation. And sometimes I'll draw in it or add a blossom that I've carefully pressed. Like my writing desk, my journal is filled with memories and things that are precious to me.

In journaling about my long marriage, I have written in each chapter about something that is close to me, something in the natural world. A nautilus shell calls forth our first kiss in the middle of the azalea bushes in Bellagio, Italy. A maple leaf takes me still further back, to my childhood in Briarcliff Manor outside New York City. Sunflowers here on the hillside about the Lake of Geneva urge me to look outward. While pieces of sea glass from Cranberry Island, off the coast of Maine, remind me to look inward. Evergreen ivy close to our front door shows me how to keep growing through the different seasons of love. My childhood pond is a lesson in Zen and wellbeing. And the giant oak reminds me to first celebrate the humble acorn.

Brenda Ueland, in her classic *If You Want to Write*, says, "Writing is a wonderful blessing, if you will use it. You will become happier, more enlightened, impassioned..." To become the happier person, write your own love story. Write journal entries and share them with your partner. Celebrate together your lasting love.

Nautilus Shell (1)   *Nautilus Shell (2)*

CHAPTER ONE

Courtship: Two Sides of the Nautilus Shell

Bellevue, October 10

In front of me on my desk sits a shell, a chambered nautilus, that leads me back to long-ago memories of courtship and lovemaking. On its rounded back, the colors—ivory, beige, coral, and black—spiral to the center. When I turn it over to the underside, I see the open pathway down which my memories continue to flow.

This morning as I write, I return to a recent memory when for my birthday Pierre and I went for the weekend to a hotel on the lake of Geneva at Montreux, known for its mini-Mediterranean climate, with palm trees, flowering laurel, azaleas.

I remember the large lovely room, the king-size bed, everything was soft white—the bedding, the curtains, the walls—with touches of royal blue—the carpet, the throw-on pillows, the two armchairs. Double windows overlooked the lake and the Alps beyond. I remember our long, slow hours in the morning as the sunlight filled the room.

There was courtship and lovemaking that kept us close during the weekend. We took time to look at each other, to talk to each other, to listen to each other. We enjoyed long walks along the lake side, quiet walks, resting by moments—alone, surrounded by flowers—and watching one of the large cruise boats sail by.

The last afternoon we boarded one of the cruise ships for a two-hour ride around the far end of Lac Leman. We found two wooden deck chairs in the very front of the boat. There was little wind. We watched the small ports and lake towns go by, behind them in the distance the Jura Mountains. Then as the boat turned to the other side, we saw the snow-covered Alps. The sun was warm on our faces. Pierre's hand was warm as he held mine.

Now here at my desk, remembering and writing in my journal, I look out my window. The patches of blue sky have widened. The gray clouds have moved aside. It will be a good day. Another day to love each other.

MEMORIES OF EARLY COURTING

OUR LOVE STORY BEGINS WITH A KISS AND ENDS WITH A promise that lasting love is possible. So I start with courtship, past and present, perhaps the most essential steps to a lasting relationship. Jalaluddin Rumi, the thirteenth-century Persian poet and Sufi mystic, wrote, "Let the beauty we love be what we do. There are one hundred ways to kneel and kiss the ground." I write here about a few of the hundred ways to court the person we love. A few of the hundred memories of our courtship. Memories that are to be springboards for your memories, for remembering moments of your courtship.

Pierre and I have been courting one another for over half a century. Courtship is often defined as a period that precedes marriage. Instead, I see courtship lasting as long as the relationship lasts. Courting is seducing. Jeremiah in The Old Testament cries out to Yahweh, "You have seduced me, Lord, and I let myself be seduced." (Jeremiah 20:7) Jeremiah the prophet has been seduced by Yahweh. We can also use these words to describe our relationship to the one we love. We let ourselves be seduced.

One night as I happened to look at my husband entering the shower, his sturdy naked back of seventy-five years summoned memories of our courtship. The memories slid down his back, leading me to still earlier memories, to the first discovery of our physical longing for one another. I relived it. I watched him as he stood in the shower, his bare arms, his strong legs. I watched him until he closed the curtain. I relived the memory as I once lived it more than fifty years ago. I longed anew for my husband. I wanted his bare arms around me, his strong legs against mine.

This memory came back to me when I was writing about a nautilus shell that I recently found in my wicker basket of little treasures. The shell is empty. Its nocturnal animal shed its home years ago, but the pathway followed by the animal is visible. The shell fits comfortably in my hand. On one side the colors spiral from black to coral to white. Turned over, its rounded back cupped in my palm, the shell looks undressed. Vulnerable. Its large orifice opens to the chambers within, each chamber more hidden. I place the shell on the shelf of my writing desk, its underbelly hidden from view.

Memories flowed down the ancient path of my shell as they flowed down the naked back of my husband. Our first kiss in the middle of azalea blossoms. We were on a student trip from the University of Grenoble to Venice. On the way home we stopped at Bellagio on Lago di Como. We took a boat across the lake to Villa Carlotta where the azaleas were in full bloom. It was Pentecost weekend, in mid-May. We walked down shaded paths, set out in spiral patterns, into a whirl of red, pink, and fuchsia azaleas. Somehow in the maze of all the blossoms, Pierre and I found ourselves alone. The bushes, their branches laden with flowers, were taller than we. They opened their arms, then closed them behind us. Pierre bent down and lifted up my face. I still taste the sweetness.

After that first kiss at the Villa Carlotta, we spent long hours together back in Grenoble at the university. Only one month remained before I was to return to the States. We talked away the hours getting to know one another, having lunch at the student dining room, lingering over a *café filtre* at our favorite café, riding up into the mountains on his scooter, a picnic in his backpack, sharing stories of our childhoods, our hopes for the future. Our friends saw that something had changed. We thought we gave no signs of our newly discovered love, but our friends said it was the way we looked at each other. I would like to think that this is still true today.

Back then we wondered, will we always look at each other this special way, with rainbow-tinted glasses? Will I always see Pierre so attractive, so appealing? Will I always see him in such favorable light? What was ahead of us? We barely spoke the same language. What would our families say? Each of us was a foreigner for the other's family. Would they welcome us? How could we make our relationship last? We decided to try. We would continue to share our thoughts through letters; we would choose a book to read and discuss it. In this way, we would discover whether the separation took us apart on different paths, or brought us closer together on adjoining paths. So every week for close to one year we wrote each other long letters.

French was the language of our courtship. As it would be the language of our lovemaking. It still is. Writing in French slowed me down. I took my time, an evening each week. I imagined Pierre sitting close; I felt him sitting close. I saw his eyes watching me, waiting for my words. Courtship through letter writing—describing my days, my commute to the city for work, a bike ride over to the Hudson to watch the sunset, my thoughts about the book we had chosen, *The Seven Storey Mountain*, by the Trappist monk, Thomas Merton. Each of us wrote about the passages that touched us. And about how much we missed each other. Even with the ocean between us, our courtship continued. Then in July, after almost a year, I flew back to France.

I remember traveling by train from Paris to Grenoble— the rolling green countryside, the tucked-away villages, then the rising mountains. I stared out the window. It had been so long since I'd seen him. Now soon he would be there. What would I feel? Would it be the same? My family and friends had questioned me. Why a Frenchman? Surely you're not serious. The train slowed down, then stopped. Pierre was waiting on the station platform. We rushed into each other's arms. Stunned, we stood there as one, until we were the last to find our way to the street. One month later, we were engaged.

We had one year to court one another before our marriage. Pierre was in New York City at Columbia, living in a university dormitory. I was teaching in Katonah High School, living with my parents in our home. Our weeks were lived separately, but our weekends we lived together, either in the city where I would stay with girlfriends from college or at home where Pierre would sleep in the den. Rules were unspoken but strict. We kissed whenever we could and longed to kiss more. But we had our whole lives to court. We did not want the flourish of first love to diminish.

Year after year we looked for ways to make ourselves attractive to one other, little ways during the day to seduce. "What color sweater would you like me to wear?" I'd ask. I wanted to dress for Pierre. I wanted him to see me attractive and appealing. I still do. I still ask him, What looks best? And I wanted him to look good. To look good for me and for everyone else. I recall a recent writers' conference when he was walking across the quad at Yale with one of our friends. Two tall, lanky men in their seventies, same color blue shirts and khaki pants, not chosen on purpose, but both looking so good. This counts. It is part of courting.

Seducing each other. Doing things we know the other likes. Daily habits that keep us attractive to each other. The way, for example, I smile. I know Pierre likes this. When I frown, he turns away. I have made a habit of smiling. Or the way I talk. I cannot change my accent. Pierre does not have an accent when he speaks English. But I will always sound like a New Yorker. However I can speak more slowly and I can let others talk. We both appreciate when the other remains discreet, a bit mysterious. We watch each other do this.

And when at times we've stopped looking at each other, when we've been in a slump and everything seemed wrong, what helped us, as it does still today, was a habit we adopted early in our marriage: we go out for a monthly date and take time to consider where we are in our relationship. It's a time to take stock. We set an evening aside each month when we can think through how we feel toward one another, how we are doing in our relationship. We share our good moments and our less-good moments, our desires and our disappointments. We listen deeply to one another. We have done this regularly for fifty-odd years, noting what's going well and what's not. When did we stop looking at each other? When did we forget to say I love you? When did we last have fun together? These are the questions that we still ask each other during our monthly dates. The pattern is set. We know that once a month we will take time to be attentive all over again.

Memories of courting. Memories flowing down my husband's back. How wonderful it is to go back to them, to feel again the longing for the other. And to remember that courting is two-ways: seducing and being seduced.

JOURNAL PRACTICE 1:
EARLY COURTING

Think back and remember the first moments of courtship.

- Do you remember your first kiss?

- Where were you?

- What was the setting?

- Were you outside, or were you somewhere sheltered inside?

- Were you alone, just the two of you, or were you hiding in a crowd?

- The touch of a caress. How did it feel?

- Did your partner respond?

The poet Rainer Maria Rilke gives us counsel. In his Letters to a Young Poet, *written between 1903 and 1908, Rilke is responding to a young man who has written to ask how to be a poet. "There is only one single way," Rilke writes. "Go into yourself." Go inward and write from "that treasure house of memories" that is within you.*

✿ SUGGESTION
Find an object that is dear to you, a stone or a shell, that has a special meaning for you. Something to hold on to as you start to write. Just as I hold on to my nautilus shell. Touching an object that is close and dear to you awakens memories and images. The memories and images revive the emotions that

were yours at the time. It's these emotions that will carry over to your present lives. Let the stone or shell lead you back to a first kiss.

Remember the words of Rilke, "Go into yourself." Close your eyes. Let the memory find you. What memory wants to be shared? Bring it to light.

Now take paper and pen, and write about your first kiss in a journal entry. Start with the date and place, and then "I am writing about courtship. I remember when we were alone..." Write for ten minutes, one or two paragraphs, not more than a short page.

Then perhaps find a moment to share the memory with your partner. If this seems difficult, there is no hurry. Whatever you discover in writing will enrich your relationship.

MEMORIES OF LOVEMAKING

I CONTINUE MY PAGES ABOUT COURTSHIP WITH memories of lovemaking. On our honeymoon, courting and lovemaking—the two sides of my nautilus shell, the visible spiral and the hidden underbelly—came together. Pierre and I courted and made love. We entered into the lovemaking as apprentices, young and willing. We were apprentices in the ancient art of alchemy, learning to find the gold. In the engravings of centuries past, we see a man and a woman heating the alchemical furnace to transform base metals into gold. They are a pair, working side by side, trying to turn lead into gold. So were we, husband and wife, as we entered the furnace, looking for the bits of gold in our lovemaking.

Another memory flows down the path of my nautilus shell, this time of our first lovemaking. It's the 1950s when many of us remained in the dark about making love. Pierre and I learned together how to give and how to receive. There was astonishment as we discovered one another. It was the first night of our honeymoon. We had just one week. It was Easter vacation. Pierre was studying, and I was teaching at a high school north of New York City. After the wedding, the reception, the dinner, the drive, we were at last alone in our hotel room. I remember the flowered wall paper and the matching flowered bedspread—red, pink, and fuchsia, the same colors as the azaleas that May afternoon at the Villa Carlotta on Lago di Como, the afternoon of our first kiss.

Pierre picked me up in his arms, and we lay down together on the bed of azaleas.

The rest of that memory belongs to the hidden, vulnerable side of the nautilus shell. The side that I turn over on the shelf of my writing desk. The underbelly of the shell from where flow our memories. Of course, young and passionate, we did not think of ourselves as alchemists, nor did we imagine ourselves making love in an alchemical furnace. But as unknowing ardent apprentices, we were learning together how to prepare the fire and how to enter it. The embers were hot.

In the months and years that followed, as the fire started to burn low, we learned how to rekindle it and then to re-enter again. Alchemy is an ongoing process. Over the years, as our relationship evolved, our lovemaking evolved. Still today, after fifty-five years of marriage, we continue to look for ways to rekindle the fires of our lovemaking. Simple ways, a long morning in bed, maybe a lazy afternoon resting in the warm sun in our backyard, And more special ways, a dinner and night out somewhere, no phones, no messages, feeling utterly alone with one another.

Going together into the furnace. It is here where Pierre and I discovered our nudity, both physical and spiritual. We let go of our trappings, of all that encumbered us—our pride and inflated egos as well as our clothes. We accepted our nakedness and opened ourselves to each other and to the unfamiliar. The fire awakens Eros, the Greek God of love, named Cupid in Roman mythology. Those he touched with his arrows were smitten. Love-struck. So it was for Pierre and me. We were love-struck.

We tried to get rid of our false prudery. We let ourselves be seen. I was shy. So was he. Together we learned to appreciate the beauty of the human body. I remember how often in a museum, I admired a sculpture—the strength of a man's torso, the taut muscles of his legs—wanting to run my hand over the marble curvature. Then seeing and touching the same curve on Pierre's body as we lay close in bed. I remember how it first felt to touch and be touched. I want to continue to feel this. And to be open and candid enough to talk about it. So that together we grow always more attentive to the other's physical desires and to our own.

In lovemaking we reveal ourselves as we are. I do not always wake up ready to embrace the morning or my dear husband. Worries and disappointments may weigh on me, may make me distant, temperamental, low-spirited. I have learned to say so—to tell Pierre that my mind is elsewhere, that I am worried about one of our children, about something I said, to ask him to be patient with me. We know this will pass. So it is for Pierre as well. When he finds himself overwhelmed with office work, he tells me. We cannot pretend with the person we love, with the person who lives day in and day out at our side. Courtship has taught us to be honest.

I learned this in the early years of our marriage. During a period of many months, while we were living in Italy, I was overwhelmed with all the children. When we first arrived in the small village of Comerio north of Milano, we had three children under five years old, and during the four years we lived there, we had two more. Each desired and planned for—a large family, we wanted a large family. But my body was exhausted. I no longer felt Pierre's caresses. I was numb. I spoke to someone I trusted—a priest—about my unease and discomfort, and he suggested that I bluff it. He won't know, he tried to assure me. After a few attempts at play acting, of course Pierre knew. At least this made me be honest and reveal the cause of my distress. We relaxed, found pleasure just being close, until I once again was alive in my body. A lesson learned, no bluffing in our lovemaking.

As I write, I realize how much we helped each other learn to give pleasure and to receive pleasure. I return to my nautilus shell and to another memory, a vacation, three days together, just the two of us, when our children were still young, on the seaside. It was our holiday, our little honeymoon. Pierre wanted to spend the morning making love and then go to the beach. I wanted to enjoy the beach, the water, the sea in the morning and make love in the evening. We settled on a long love nap in the afternoon. The compromise sounds easy, but it is not always so. We returned to being apprentices, the two of us, both learning to make time for lovemaking—time to court one another, time to seduce one another.

Often Pierre and I did not find the right moment. Distractions, discouragements intervened. And there were periods when we had to forego making love and look for other ways to express our desire. Times imposed by ill health, by birth control, pregnancies. Times that let us learn the sway and heat of just a caress. There were periods where one of us pulled back from lovemaking. When the other did not understand. When we were not getting along well, when we felt the other was not making an effort to understand, when our anger was stronger than the arrows of Eros.

We looked for ways to quiet down and listen to each other. From early in our marriage we looked for ways to stoke the alchemical fire. The bits and pieces of lead do not overnight become gold. The flame needs to burn. We needed to understand what was happening, where we were in our relationship. Our monthly dates, the setting aside a time to do this, were helping us. Each month I noted some of our thoughts, a few lines for Pierre, a few lines for me, and a few for us. This way the next month we would look back and see where we were and where we wanted to be.

This is how we came to know that after the storm, there is sunshine. And through courting and loving, something new is born. Pierre and I welcomed this process, first on the physical level with the successive births of our children—the miraculous experience of witnessing the birth of each one. The births were natural, without anesthesia, and they were painful. Each time I wanted to be fully conscious and each time I thought I would not succeed in bringing forth this new child. The baby was too huge, the pain was too huge. Pierre stood at my side. And then, together we witnessed the extraordinary eruption of new life.

A memory. Our first child was born in southern France. The delivery was very long, lasting a night and a day and a night. The doctor went home. The midwife literally pushed the baby down and out. Afterwards, in my hospital room, as I rested with the baby at my breast, Pierre squeezed cool drops of fresh orange juice onto my parched lips, onto my tongue. It was ambrosia. We were now three. And this incredible gift of new life was repeated with each child, a taste of immortality as we welcomed each birth.

This something new is also born on the psychological level with the birth of a deeper consciousness. A new awareness. With successive lovemaking, Pierre and I entered into an ever new *coniunctio*, the Jungian word for a deep union. We grew more conscious of the other's presence and learned together the language of lovemaking. We tried to accord our bodies, to be in tune like violinists in a duet. In continuing to look for the same pitch, we have grown in patience and in tenderness, a tenderness that intensifies our lovemaking.

As I write about lovemaking, I think about how the *yin*, the welcoming, often seen as the female, and the *yang*, the giving, seen as the male, fit together not only within each of us, but within our relationship. Pierre is not only the *yang*, the giving, but also the *yin*, the welcoming. And I have to remember that I am not only *yin*, the welcoming, but also *yang*, giving.

In fitting the *yin* and the *yang* together, we observed that when the setting changes, so does the mood of our lovemaking. We looked for different places. I remember making love in a dense thicket of trees near the coast in northern France, where there were only wild rabbits and us. The natural setting—the windswept trees, the low scrubs—still makes this memory special.

It is the same when the time of day changes. When we went to bed, tired and worn-out, we were no longer making love at night. Nor in the morning as we awoke with thoughts of the work ahead of us. So then it was in the middle of the day that we stopped our usual routine and sought each other. It was a time of day when our senses were most alive.

Yin and *yang*, remembering how well we fit together.

JOURNAL PRACTICE 2:
LOVEMAKING

_____

Recall a time when you felt very close to your partner or spouse. When your desire was reawakened.

- How long ago was it?

- What were your surroundings?

- Are the colors still sharp or have they faded?

- What time of day was it?

- Was there sunshine or were you in the shadows?

- Were you standing, or sitting? Or lying down?

- Were you caught by surprise or was it planned?

Rilke continues to advise the would-be poet, "Think, dear sir, of the world you carry within you." You have a whole world within you. A world of submerged images and sensation of your past. Rilke tells the poet to turn his attention there. "Be attentive to that which rises up in you." These images are waiting for you to write about them.

❧ SUGGESTION

Writing opens the door to the world within you. With each memory that rises, as you write about it, more memories will rise, letting you see more clearly where you are in your life, in your relationship. Previously, you wrote about the memory of a first kiss. Return to your stone or shell that you found and hold it again in your hand. It is inviting you now to revisit your memory of lovemaking. Close your eyes and remember. Feel again the warmth of the moment. Let yourself be courted. And court the other.

Starting with the date and the place, write a short journal entry about the experience. "I am writing about lovemaking. I remember the place when we found one another..." Enjoy ten minutes of writing and remembering.

Afterwards, maybe remember the experience together with your partner. And think about the days ahead. How, in the midst of all you are doing, can you find new moments for courtship?

MEMORIES OF HONEYMOONS
AND SHARED PASTIMES

In thinking back, I see how both courting and lovemaking were fully lived on our honeymoon. A honeymoon is so called in order to describe the days just after the wedding when we are told that the moments are the sweetest, the honey-filled moments. There is the implication here that the sweet moments will wane like the moon. And it is true that after several years, there were times when we felt our attraction for each other diminishing. But these became times for other honeymoons.

While raising our large family, Pierre and I looked for weekends to go away, just the two of us, once or twice a year. We asked friends or family to take care of our children and we reciprocated. We chose a place where we could give ourselves fully to each other. To look and listen, to taste again the sweetest moments. Our annual honeymoons rekindled the fire of our mutual attraction. They became part of our courtship.

I remember a weekend in an old priory in France, in the Drôme, at Sainte Cécile. It was late November, cold, windy, and stormy. And our relationship at that point was also cold, windy, and stormy. We left on a Friday after Pierre's work, a three-hour drive, barely speaking to each other. We arrived exhausted, wondering if it was worth it, ready to turn around and go home. There was a wood fire burning in the large open fireplace. We sat down on a comfortable sofa with a glass of Muscadet wine and warmed ourselves. The rest of the weekend was a love feast. In remembering it, I want to return, to taste again the sweetness of the Muscadet. The hours spent making love in our monastic room, the smallish bed—like all matrimonial beds in France—with heavy damask sheets, the thick stone walls, the quiet.

Still today, even though we are alone at home, we go away from time to time for a short honeymoon. Recently we went for three days to the family chalet in the French Alps not far from Geneva where we live, but far enough to feel ourselves disconnected from our busy lives at home. Each morning we went for a walk in the valley, alongside a rushing mountain stream, looked up at the silver cascades falling down the mountain sides into the ice cold creek. The afternoons, after a lazy, slow lunch outside, we napped and lay close to each other, without our cell phones and computers. Complete rest, letting us look forward to a couple's date in the evening, refreshed, in love, ready to talk and listen to each other.

❧

Another way we keep our courtship alive is to enjoy shared pastimes. This awakens attraction, a desire to seduce and to be seduced. The first pastime that comes to mind is dancing. Pierre tangos beautifully. I sometimes say I fell in love dancing the tango in Grenoble. He leads superbly, and I learned to follow. In the first days, we danced at the student balls, we danced with friends at cafés, we danced alone in my boarding house. One year later, after I'd left and then returned to France for the summer, we danced anew, our bodies alert to each other, alert to the rhythm of seduction.

Then in the States, while Pierre was at Columbia and I was teaching, we danced on weekends at a nearby restaurant, Tappen Hill, above Tarrytown, where there was a circular dance floor and on Saturday evenings a few musicians. When we asked for a tango, we were often the only ones dancing but we paid attention only to each other. After our wedding, on our short honeymoon, we took my small record player and Pierre's records to the inn in Virginia. When we weren't making love, we were dancing.

Today we still look for opportunities to dance—a special celebration, a wedding, a family or class reunion, a village festival, an open-air concert. But most often, it's just the two of us, alone at home, dancing for a few minutes in the evening before we sit down to dinner. Dancing a very slow tango to a favorite Paganini recording. The music alone puts us in the mood for courting, for enjoying just being together.

Another activity that brings us together, that gives us time to appreciate each other's company, is walking. There are family walks that we did with our children and there are couple walks that just the two of us do. I am writing about the latter. A couple's walk is like a couple's date. We look for quiet roads and paths where we will be alone in the middle of trees, plants, flowers. We walk side by side and catch glimpses of each other, pacing our steps together, feeling the same rhythm. We stop and surprise each other in a moment's close embrace.

Pierre and I are fortunate to live in beautiful countryside— near the lake or near the mountains or even right close to home. We often walk up the street where we live, beyond the railroad tracks, along a shaded lane, and into open fields, bordered by woods. We know our way by heart and have time to look around us. We point out to one another the bright yellows in a bed of tulips, the stones in a brook shining in the shaded sunlight. Or we lift our eyes and look together at the shape of a cloud.

There is a walnut tree not far away and come September we try to be among the first to look for the fallen nuts on the ground. Pierre reaches up to shake a few low branches. Then he takes a stick to hit higher branches. We fill our pockets. I have never tasted fresh walnuts. Pierre remembers a walnut tree in the backyard of his parents' house. As a child, during the war, with rationing and food shortages, the walnuts were a treat. I listen and try to imagine. A single walnut tree and a whole story. The fresh walnuts that we have gathered taste less bitter.

There is also our shared love of travel. New places, new cultures, new sights, tastes, and smells. Living in Switzerland, we travel easily around Europe. We traveled with the children, wanting them to share our love of discovering unknown places, unknown lands. We took them to Yugoslavia, eight of us in our Peugeot station wagon, during the time when Tito was still holding the country together. We were tourists ahead of the times, vacationing on the coast of Croatia, swimming in the Adriatic Sea. It was also during the time when three of us could sit up front in the car, then another three and the last two behind. It was a long drive.

When the children left home, Pierre and I were able to take lengthier trips. We traveled to Vietnam to discover the country of our youngest child. In Saigon we visited the orphanage, Phu My, where our son spent the first two years of his life. We looked at photos of hundreds of young children who were flown away to adoptive families in Europe and America during the long, terrible years of the war. We added a photo I had in my purse. It was taken the day after Daniel's arrival in Geneva; he is surrounded by his five new siblings. He is dressed in orange—an orange jumper suit and a white and orange striped T-shirt—and he is sitting in the middle of the floor in his small room. His brothers and sisters encircle him, fascinated by their new little brother, each wanting to make him smile, each wanting to welcome him, each wanting to love him.

Memories of travel and courtship continue to flow along the path of my nautilus shell. Not so long ago while in the States, we visited a poet friend and his artist wife in St. Petersburg, on the Gulf coast. We stayed in their fisherman's cottage, very close to the water. We could hear the sea from our bedroom window. We could smell it, we could taste it. We have a photo that our friend's wife took of us, in each other's arms, with the sun setting behind us, beyond the bay and the Gulf of Mexico. There is a golden light illuminating our outlines. When we look at the photo today, we feel anew how close we were, how warm and protected we felt, there, over four thousand miles away from home. There is a copy of the photo in Pierre's office and another one in my study. I look at it often and each time I ask myself, was it taken yesterday?

As I write these pages, I share my writing with Pierre. I read him a few pages of my chapter, and we go back together to memories of our first kiss in Bellagio, our first night of lovemaking, the birth of our first child and the fresh orange juice, the love scene in the woods with the wild rabbits, dancing the tango at Tappen Hill alone on the dance floor, our September walks to the single walnut tree, the glass of Muscadet and the open fire in the large hearth in the Drôme, the vacation in Tito's Yugoslavia with the children, and the vacation on the Gulf coast, the setting sun.

Remembering these warm moments renews our desire for one another. We think about creating new moments, new opportunities for courtship. Things we can do together, places we can go to, lazy afternoons in our backyard, more long walks along the lake, evenings out to a concert. Monthly dates, yearly honeymoons. Enjoying each other's company. Taking time to look at one another, time to listen to one another.

It's all part of courtship. Of growing in love. Of never stepping into the same river twice. Of letting the beauty of lovemaking renew itself. I have used in this chapter the word seduce. It's a strong word and a true word for courting and loving. I still want to seduce Pierre, and I still want to be seduced. So it is for Pierre as well. He wants to seduce me and he wants to be seduced. As we age, if we continue to pay attention both to ourselves and to the other, our courting will continue to ripen. We will find ways to love and be loved into our eighties and maybe still into our nineties.

The journal of our marriage, the notes from our monthly dates, will show us the path. The path to finding the bits of gold in our relationship. Apprentices for life in courting and lovemaking.

JOURNAL PRACTICE 3:
A FAVORITE PASTIME

Go back in your memory to one particular moment of a favorite, shared pastime where you especially enjoyed the presence of your partner, the pleasure of being together.

- When was it?
- What were you doing?
- Were there just the two of you?
- Did you stop to look at each other?
- Did you reach for each other?
- What emotion was the strongest?
- Did you share it?

Rainer Maria Rilke writes to reassure the young poet, "New clarity will come," he promises, but only to those who are patient. Just as the tree stands firm in the storms of spring, knowing summer will come, so must the writer stand firm, knowing words will come. "I learn it daily," Rilke writes. "Patience is everything."

⚘ SUGGESTION

In writing these pages, do not rush. Be patient with yourself. You are taking time for yourself and for your relationship. Don't try to write the "perfect" journal entry. There is no perfect journal entry. There are no rules. Each journal is unique, each journal entry is unique. You are writing about a personal experience. You are looking inward. Tiptoe into your memory. You are bringing to light the memory of an experience. It will find its own expression.

Write another journal entry about a special moment that drew you together. "I am remembering one of our walks together. We were walking along the..." Find the bright colors, the smells. Let them bring you renewed happiness.

When the time comes, share what you are writing with your partner. Maybe make a couple's date. Go somewhere, a place you both like, where you both are comfortable. Read the pages together. Re-create the experience and feel again the happiness to be together.

Then, if you wish, put the pages in a journal. Give them a title, "Memories of Courtship". You are writing your love story.

Maple Leaf in Dish

CHAPTER TWO

Commitment: The Story of the Maple Leaf

Geneva, October 11

On my walk this morning, in the midst of all the fallen autumn leaves, I thought about the red maple leaf I picked up a year ago on a walk with Pierre—the leaf that I write about in the following chapter. A close to perfect one with the five lobes intact. I brought it home and put it in a plain earthenware dish to appreciate for the rest of the day. I wanted to find another one today, but the early morning rain messed them up. They all looked weather beaten and tattered.

As I write this journal entry, I am thinking that Pierre and I might also look weather beaten and tattered. There have been rainstorms. Thunderstorms and lightning. But the sunshine has prevailed.

We have been married fifty-five years. I add up the days, 20,075. I cannot not believe this, over 20,000 days and nights together. I could take away a few each month when Pierre was traveling, but the number is still staggering. We slept together 20,000 times. And we are still in love.

This is what I am writing about in SIDE BY SIDE. *How to make a long relationship work. I have identified seven steps, there are certainly many more. It's the first two steps, courtship and commitment—that have made possible the 20,000 days and nights. During the rainstorms, I sometimes questioned my commitment. Why should I stay thousands of miles from my "home" in the States?*

Because I made a commitment to love Pierre. And because he made a commitment to love me.

It's this mutual commitment that has kept us together, along with courtship that has kept the love embers glowing. Already during our year at Grenoble, there were early seeds of a growing commitment. I remember the long hours we spent listening to each other. As we got to know one another, we learned to trust each other.

This is what I want to suggest to the reader. To go back in memory to moments of commitment, to early memories of listening to each other. To find the memory and write about it in a short journal entry as I am doing here. And to think about how to renew those early pledges of love.

I still think about this. How can Pierre and I renew our vows? Not formally, though this, too, is possible. We could look ahead to do this for our next important wedding anniversary. But today I am thinking about renewing them informally. Like every day. Like wishing each other a happy day as we sit down for breakfast.

Whether the maple leaves are weather-beaten or bright red perfect, they will remind me tomorrow morning to tell Pierre I love him and to wish him a good day.

SEEDS OF COMMITMENT

THE SECOND COMPONENT OF LASTING LOVE, ONE THAT
Pierre and I feel is as important as courtship, is our commitment
to our marriage. Kahlil Gibran wrote, "To wake at dawn with
a winged heart and give thanks for another day of loving." To
wake each morning saying yes to our love. We cannot do this
without a mutual commitment. Without saying, I do. As we did
the day we married. Memories of commitment, pledges of love.

To lead me back to memories of commitment, I choose
a maple leaf. When Pierre and I go for walks, I often pick up
something—a maple leaf, a wild daisy, a small stone. When
there are many maple leaves, many daisies, many stones, they
all look alike. But when I pick up only one, hold it in my hand,
and look at it closely, it is unique. It reminds me that each of
us is unique. That our relationship is unique. And that we are
committed to keeping it alive and flourishing.

Memory. It was late September. Pierre and I were coming
back from a long walk past the vineyards and down to the
lakeside. We were talking about the months ahead. Freshly
fallen leaves bordered the road. We were close to our house,
near the two maple trees that turn bright red early in the fall. A
burst of crimson, shining in the sunlight. I picked up a brilliant
red leaf with the five lobes intact and a few tar spots near the
stem.

I want to hold onto this image. Meister Eckhart, the
thirteenth-century theologian, writes, "When the soul wants

to experience something, she throws out an image in front of her and then steps into it." To throw out an image. And then to step into it. Writers do this in their work. I ask my students to do this, to close their eyes and see what image surfaces on the screen of their imagination. Then to write about it and see where it leads them. I am always surprised by the stories that follow. In this second chapter, I let the red maple leaf lead me as I write about commitment.

The leaf takes me back to my childhood, in Briarcliff Manor, outside New York City, to the maple trees in the woods beyond our dead-end road. Each fall I would look for brightly colored maple leaves, a few small ones, with their five lobes fully intact. I would dip the leaves into melted wax and place them carefully in a large scrapbook. The scrapbooks have disappeared but the memories remain.

I can go back still further, to the farm where I lived the first years of my life, on Croton Dam Road, in Ossining, to the wide expanse of fields and dark wooden fences, the maple trees that turned bright red each fall and the white horses looking for high grass and shade. I played for hours in those golden fields, content and carefree, climbing along the fences, feeding apples to the horses. I would hold out my hand as flat as I could and wait for the fat wet lips of the horse to scoop it up. As I remember this, I feel a commitment to the role of memory itself. My childhood becomes again alive and vibrant, giving me security and confidence in who I am.

Pierre does not remember much of his childhood. The big house in northern France, already two brothers and two sisters, a strict upbringing, formal family gatherings—obeying in rows, sitting in rows, standing in rows. Then the war, the evacuation, driving to southern France with a mattress on the top of the car as protection against the strafing of the German planes low overhead. The chaos and confusion, until his parents found another big house in Annemasse, which was then still in the free zone of France, near Geneva. He does not want to remember going to boarding school when he was only eight years old. Taking the train home alone even after the Germans arrived and occupied the area. At the boarding school, there were no fields to play in, no maple trees to climb. No bright leaves to gather and save in a scrapbook. The winters were long and cold and dark. Pierre is only now returning to a few childhood memories and beginning to find the words to write about them.

Back to our walk and the maple leaf. When we arrived home from our walk, I put my red leaf in a small dish on the kitchen table. The small dish is another image that calls forth memories. The dish comes from the monastery where I often go for a day or an afternoon of quiet ever since we moved to Geneva forty years ago. The nuns make earthenware pottery, and most times I bring home a dish, a bowl, a mug. Once I brought home a water jug which became a lesson in vulnerability when a crack appeared on its smooth surface several years later. It's a story I have written about in earlier books, a story I continue to learn from.

The water jug survived a car accident, when we rolled over twice—the car, the water jug, and myself. Only years later did the crack appear, starting to work its way upward through the rings of clay. The crack was inside the jug, making the jug vulnerable. Writing about it led me to realize that the same crack is inside us. We, too, are vulnerable. So is our relationship. Pierre and I need to remember this and to keep our sense of commitment strong. To love one another "until death do us part." The water jug continues to sit on our kitchen table. Each morning it reminds me to pay attention to the crack. I am vulnerable. A lifelong gift from the monastery.

The monastery is on the top of Mont Voirons, an hour's drive from our house, along the lake of Geneva and then up the mountain in neighboring France. In earlier years it was the home of Dominican monks. The foundations of their earlier monastery are embedded on the mountainside. Before the Dominicans, many centuries before, a temple to Jupiter crowned the mountain. The ground is drenched with centuries of prayer.

I think back to the last time I went up to the monastery. Pierre was with me. We walked in the woods to a small, very old chapel where there is a statue of the Black Madonna that has welcomed me over the years, my joys and thanksgiving, and also my tears and sorrows. Somehow her darkness released my misgivings and fears. This time the two of us sat quietly, bringing to mind thoughts and wishes for each other and for our children and grandchildren. Back in the large monastery church, we stayed for vespers, with the *petites soeurs* in their light beige prayer robes, thirty to forty little sisters, most of them young, sitting up front.

On the way home, we talked about our faith, about what still today takes us up the mountain to the monastery. In recent years our regular Sunday churchgoing is no longer automatic. Out spirituality has become more personal and less traditional. Pierre comes from a traditional French Catholic family. He grew up reciting the rosary, kneeling in front of the family's statue of the Virgin Mary, with his siblings and parents. He was the oldest son in a family of ten children. I grew up in a family of two children, my older sister and me. There were no statues of Mary in our home or in our Congregational church where our family worshipped. Pierre and I continue to work hard to bridge our different backgrounds of faith.

When we met at Grenoble University, I was an American graduate student looking for something deeper in my life, looking to understand an older culture that somehow held me in its grip. Pierre was finishing engineering school, after long years at a Jesuit preparatory school. He was looking for freedom, for independence. I was intrigued by all his years of traditional upbringing and his brooding Catholic faith. He was intrigued by my fresh inquisitive spirit. We would stay for hours in the student lounge or at the Café la Grenette, asking each other questions and sharing stories of our childhoods. I liked the way Pierre listened, the way he didn't take his gray eyes off mine. He still listens to me this way. I spoke slowly, looking for my words in French. Pierre waited, listening. Attentive.

By the end of the school year at Grenoble, after our first kiss in the azalea gardens of the Villa Carlotta in May, we were spending time together almost every day. The date of my departure was drawing close. It would be two more years before we committed ourselves to marriage. But already there were early seeds of commitment, pledges of trust as we continued to open our hearts and listen to one another.

Our sharing often circled back to our faith in all that was good in creation. When we looked around us, what we saw was good. What we saw was just. We wanted our lives to be part of what we both sensed was an ongoing current of love. We didn't use these words. We were young, striving to express our desire to give meaning to our lives, asking ourselves if we could do so together.

These early seeds of commitment were grounded in our belief in something bigger than ourselves. In our Judeo-Christian tradition, we call this something God. Embracing other traditions, we may call this source Love. "God is love... wherever there is love, there is God." Both of our faiths have evolved over the years, but our commitment to this higher—deeper—source of being has remained. Throughout these pages, as throughout our lives, there is an undertow that continues to pull Pierre and me toward this greater being, to this God of love. It is an undertow that has confronted violent countercurrents, but that has given us day-by-day strength to say yes to life, yes to our love.

The seeds that were planted during the early years of our marriage would grow and blossom as the years turned into decades. And as today, I stay amazed to think that we have loved and lived together for over fifty-five years.

All this from a maple leaf.

JOURNAL PRACTICE 4:
SEEDS OF COMMITMENT

Do you have a memory of when you and your partner first deeply listened to one another?

- Where were you?

- What made you listen to the other?

- What stories did you share?

- Did you look at each other a special way?

- What emotions did you feel?

- Was there already a pledge of trust?

- Do you remember what you said?

In this chapter, let's turn to Brenda Ueland and her book, If You Want to Write, *first published in 1938 and still in print today. Ueland assures us that we all have stories to share and the creative talent to write them. "Everybody is talented, original and has something important to say." When we write from our true self, each of us has something original and important to say. Self-trust, Ueland writes, is one of the most important things in writing.*

❧ SUGGESTION
It is in journaling that we learn to write from our true self. When you journal, it is helpful to discover the time of day when you are most ready to write. When you feel relaxed and

can look forward to sitting down for ten minutes with pen and paper. It's helpful also to discover the place where you are most ready to write. Wherever you are most comfortable—at your desk, at the kitchen table, in a café.

Let your journal writing be playful and enjoyable. Remember, you have something important to say. You have your love story to write.

Sit down. Relax all your muscles. Feel your pen in your hand. When you are ready, start to write, just ten minutes. Describe the memory of early listening, of an early seed of commitment. "I remember when we spent a long time just listening to each other..." Write what happened. Write slowly.

Look to share your short page with your partner or spouse. Together, remember when you truly listened to one another.

COMMITMENT TO EACH OTHER
AND TO OUR CHILDREN

MY RED LEAF TAKES ME BY THE HAND. I SEE ITS CENTRAL vein as representing our commitment to this source of being, this God of love. From this vein, the five lobes reach out like five fingers, pointing to other commitments in our marriage. The central one is the largest—our commitment to each other. It is a choice that Pierre and I make each day. Mostly we do it unconsciously, just happy to be together. Other times, we make an effort. We train ourselves to see all that is good in the other.

What do I love the most about Pierre? I remember the passage in the New Testament, "Whatever is pure, whatever is lovely, whatever is gracious, if there is any excellence, if there is anything worthy of praise, think upon these things." (Philippians 4:8).

When I think about all that I love in Pierre, what I don't love has less importance. I love his interest in me, his interest in the world around him. I love the conversations we have, just the two of us, and the conversations we have with those around us, with family and friends, even with strangers. I love less his sometimes rigid attitude, patterned on his father's example. I would like him to be more flexible, more lenient. I can get worked up about this. But when I stop myself and consciously choose to look at what I love about him, I calm down and become more understanding and responsive.

It is the same for him. When he looks at what he loves about me, my welcoming smile each morning, my affectionate attention to those around me, he more easily overlooks my perfectionism, my wanting everything to be just right. He patiently waits while I check every detail in preparing a dinner for friends. And when I ask him at the last moment to help me polish the silver, if I remember to smile, together we end up enjoying even the task of making the silver shine.

Our commitment to each other makes us want the best for the other. I want to ensure comfort and happiness for Pierre. And I want still more to do whatever I can to help him be the fine person I love. The fine person he sometimes struggles to be. The times when he stumbles, I stay by his side. Pierre does the same for me. His love makes me a better person. When I am down, when I am discouraged, I turn to him. I know he is there.

To help us live our daily commitment to each other, I return to our monthly dates. It was in our couples' group in the early years of our marriage that we first discovered the importance of a monthly review. It was not enough to enjoy sporadic moments of sharing. We needed something more regular. Once a month we set aside a time to talk about our relationship, what was going well, what was going less well. We chose the date and the place ahead of time. Like in *Le Petit Prince*, we prepared our hearts in advance. This taught us to try to save our arguments for when we were more willing to listen to one another. Our monthly dates became a practice, a habit. A monthly checkup on our relationship.

We looked for the most conducive timing and setting. When and where did we best relate to one another? This has changed over the years, but most often we go out for dinner to a quiet restaurant where there are fewer distractions than at home. And sometimes we seem to listen best when we are going for a walk. After a while, our steps fall into the same rhythm, our arms swing together. Our minds are open and receptive.

It was on such a walk, over twenty-five years back, in the Jura Mountains, older and less steep than the Alps, that Pierre asked me what I wanted to do with the rest of my life. I was turning fifty. The older children were beginning to leave home. His question stopped me short. I sat down on a stone wall close by. I was so used to talking about his professional life, about the children's busy lives, that I hadn't thought much about my own life. I didn't have an answer on the spot. But the question was planted. With time, a few months later, I found my answer. I wanted to write. I wanted to turn my journal entries, my letters, my scribbles in the margins of books, my notes from our monthly dates, into longer pieces of writing. I wanted to write short stories and personal essays, to write about falling in love with a Frenchman.

So it was that I went to my first writers' workshop as a fiftieth birthday gift. I chose a workshop on Long Island, in New York, where my mother was staying with friends after my father's death. For two weeks I went to class and wrote late into the night. Stories poured onto paper. When I returned home to Geneva, I set up a study in our youngest son's bedroom. He was still living at home and was happy to move into a bigger bedroom in the basement. Pierre understood my longing to write and shared my happiness as I released this outburst of creativity.

This was part of our commitment to each other—to be supportive of each other's desires and dreams. And as I continued along the path of a writing life, Pierre continued to encourage me. Still today he is at my side as I write this book. We look for memories together. I give him the pages to read. And often I give them again, as I continue to rewrite and polish. He notes in the margins, "Is this a new section?" or "I like this." "What do you mean?" or "Why this memory here?" and even sometimes at the top of the journal practices, "Good encouragement, I should try!"

Another lobe of my maple leaf might point to our commitment to our children. How do Pierre and I relate to our children? How do we live our commitment as parents? This is something we discuss almost every day, sharing our wishes and our regrets, wanting to look forward. Where are our children today? What are they doing? What are their needs, their wishes, their dreams? Our grandchildren enter into our discussions with the same questions. Where are they, what are they doing? Is there something we can do to help them grow with confidence into adulthood?

And once a month we sit down and talk about each child and each grandchild. One of our grandchildren is spending his junior year in Minnesota, far away from his family in

Switzerland. Is there a way to grow closer to him now that he is in the States? He is on Facebook, what can grandparents say to him? How can we enter into his chats? Should we even try?

I reflect back to when our own children were very young and remember our early discussions about how we would bring them up. With how much discipline? What would be the father's role, what would be the mother's role? This was when the sharing of our different experiences with other couples was so important. We talked through our different ideas of how children should behave. And how we as parents should behave. We listened to the other parents and this in turn made it easier to listen to each other.

In Pierre's large family in northern France, traditions held fast. He was raised in the same formal manner as his parents and his grandparents. The authority of the paternal figure was not to be questioned. Pierre addressed each of his parents with the French *vous*, not with the more familiar *tu* form, showing respect but also distance. His parents said *tu* to him, he said *vous* to them. The children did not speak at the dinner table unless they were addressed. The father was the patriarch.

I was raised in a small family living in suburbia, in a quiet friendly neighborhood. My father worked in New York City, commuting daily. My mother stayed mostly at home, volunteered at school and church, but was prone to depression. Dad rounded out the corners, always ready to read to us, to play with us—kickball on our street after supper, swimming lessons at the village pool. As the younger of two sisters by three years, I had lots of time alone to walk in the fields at the end of our road, to climb trees as high as I could, to sit on a large flat rock on the top of a hill not far from home and daydream.

We both felt we wanted to give this same liberty to our children. But would it be possible in a French environment? Would we be able to mark our own path? My family was far away, but Pierre's was close. In looking back now, I realize that our move to Belgium and then to Italy gave us the distance we needed to find our own way in bringing up our children.

And how many children would we have? Two, as in my family? Or ten as in Pierre's? From the start we wanted a big family. I remember our anticipation as we planned for each new child. We were not alone back then in having a large family. Many of our friends were expecting their fourth or fifth child. We settled for six. A compromise between ten and two which today, we realize, revealed our constant search for the middle ground.

Five children in ten years. Then opening our home to our sixth from Vietnam. Six children in fourteen years. This explains the amount of time we spent trading thoughts and reflections about how each child was doing and how we were doing as parents. I was a full-time mom, learning to adapt to other languages and cultures as we moved around Europe, following Pierre's job moves—Belgium, Italy, France, and Switzerland. But still wanting to get out of the house even for just a few hours each week, almost always finding some volunteer teaching at the local school.

Our monthly dates continued to help us and I continued to write down a few notes each time. We were keeping track, remembering where we were the previous month, where we wanted to be in the months ahead. How could I find more time in each day? How could I learn to be more patient? Pierre had his own questions. And how could we find ways to pay more attention to each other and to our children?

We were living in Geneva when we welcomed our youngest. It was in April 1974, the last year before Saigon fell. Traumatized by two years of war, bombings, hunger, and polio, he needed armfuls of attention and care. And our arms were already very full. He was not able to stand up alone. He needed a helping hand. He was not sleeping, and for months he screamed from nightmares, late into the night and early morning. Nor was he speaking. We decided to use only French at home and avoid speaking to one another in English, hoping to facilitate his ability to communicate.

As I recall these memories and write about them, I realize that Pierre and I were stretched very thin with the six children. We were stretched thin also for each other. Pierre at his work, me at home, both of us trying to be present to our children, we sometimes overlooked each other. We needed our courting and lovemaking. We needed our monthly dates and discussions to hold our family together, to remember all that was going well, and for the rest, we needed to take and discuss one problem at a time. I write this in the past tense but it is true still today. Pierre and I still need the courting and lovemaking.

The children have long since left home, but our commitment continues—including the grandchildren. We look for ways to stay close to them. It's mostly text messages. Who maybe needs a message of love? Who needs a thumbs-up? The oldest is twenty-six—our age when we married. Recently he came with his girlfriend for the weekend. The youngest grandchild is eight. She lives in Brooklyn with her older brother. We try to see these two on Skype, we listen to the brother play the trumpet while his sister dances in the background. All the other grandchildren live either in Switzerland or in France.

Wife and husband, mother and father, grandmother and grandfather. While wanting to remember our commitments—flowing from the undertow of our shared faith—we still want to remember the enjoyment of being together. These first two steps, courtship and commitment, go together and they overlap. To enjoy being in love.

JOURNAL PRACTICE 5:
COMMITMENT TO EACH OTHER

Find a memory of something you did that showed your commitment to your partner or spouse.

- What did you do?

- Is it something you do often?

- Is it a commitment that is easy to make?

- Why?

- What were your emotions?

- How did your partner respond?

- Did you talk about it?

Brenda Ueland warns against being afraid of not writing well, of putting "something down that is not as good as Shakespeare." Then it is no wonder, she writes, that we don't enjoy it. "When you write, you must feel free." Free of all the people telling you that you cannot write. The only good teachers that you have, Ueland writes, are your friends who think you are interesting and want to know more. If you don't have such a friend, imagine one.

❧ SUGGESTION

In the process of journal writing, you learn to let go of your doubts and fears about not being able to write a page. This is free writing, not worrying about your choice of words, your

COMMITMENT: THE STORY OF THE MAPLE LEAF

grammar, your sentence structure, your punctuation. Let your hand lead you. Write just ten minutes.

To help uncover early memories, find a leaf like my maple leaf. Is the leaf green, hinting of spring? What memories of spring do you have? Or is it bright yellow hinting of autumn? Let your leaf coax forth memories.

Again, note the date and the place, and start a new short entry, remembering an experience of commitment to your partner. Maybe begin again with, "I am writing about. . ." or just go right into the memory. Just ten minutes.

Does your partner remember the same moment? Share your words and appreciate the closeness and commitment anew.

PARENTS AND SIBLINGS, FRIENDS AND NEIGHBORS

I RETURN TO THE IMAGE OF MY MAPLE LEAF AND LET IT speak to me of still other commitments—to our parents and siblings, and to our friends and neighbors. Memories of how we lived these commitments and how today we continue to honor them.

First our parents. We wanted to stay close to them, but geographically we were far apart. Pierre's parents were living in Haute Savoie. My parents were living in New York and then still farther away in Arizona. And we were living in Belgium, then Italy, then Switzerland. The distance to Pierre's parents was manageable. We often went for a weekend and for longer periods during the summer holidays. The distance to America was different. While I was bringing up the children, I returned only every other year. I regretted this, for myself and for my parents. I wrote long letters each week. These letters my mother saved. They are in a trunk, the elastics that she carefully used to group them by year have broken but the dates remain on the envelopes.

Memories. My father was the first of our parents to die, just as he was turning eighty. In September that year he learned he had melanoma cancer, too much sun from his retirement years in Arizona. I traveled to be with him in November. He died in early December. The loss and grief were colossal. He always encouraged me to "go do it," to dive from the diving board in our village swimming pool when I was four years old, to hold my tennis racket tight and to return the ball. He's still there encouraging me.

Pierre's father died of heart failure when he was eighty-six. It was our turn to be spending the weekend with him and Pierre's mother. He was in the hospital. We sat next to him, speaking to him as he came in and out of a coma. When he stopped breathing, Pierre was holding his hand. This was perhaps the closest moment Pierre had with his father. With the patriarchal role of the father, there was no place for intimacy. Pierre is sorry for this and is not letting it happen with his own children.

Pierre's mother suffered from Alzheimer's the last ten years of her life. When it was our weekend to be at her side, we looked for ways to be present to her. We would take her in her wheelchair to the lounge where there was an upright piano. Pierre would play simple melodies of songs she knew as a child. For a while she listened, slightly moving her head in rhythm to the music. Then she no longer moved her head. She died quietly in her bed, closing her eyes one last time.

My mother died the same year as Pierre's mother. I spent a summer month with her just before her death. At ninety-two years old, she said she was ready to leave this world. She died shortly after I left. It was on September 11, 2001. I had a scheduled phone call to her that morning. She was not aware of what was happening in the city where she was born. Incredibly, in the midst of the tragic surreal chaos, when all air traffic ceased, when local phone service became so glutted, it shut down and no overseas lines were working, my telephone call at ten a.m. Eastern Standard time went through. I was able to say good-bye. This will remain a mystery for me—one of those moments in life that open to a deeper level of being.

Our two mothers did not know each other well, but shortly after their deaths, I saw them in a dream. They were walking toward each other, in the middle of a meadow filled with little white flowers. They turned toward me, coming to greet me. Both of them were younger, perhaps in their fifties. Both of them in long dresses, quite lovely, arms outstretched. It's a dream that I go back to and that I share with Pierre. It brings comfort.

The circles of commitment overlap. There are also our sisters and brothers, aunts and uncles, cousins. The traditional family reunions kept Pierre close to his siblings. His brothers and their spouses all live in France. We continue to meet together once a year. It's quite remarkable how we all get along. Pierre thinks that the number helps. No one wants to be a troublemaker. Whatever the reason, the sense of family remains very strong.

On my side, my older sister who lives in Virginia and I have discovered an intimacy that eluded us while we were raising our large families, separated by country, culture, and language. I look forward to our now almost annual visits, either in the States or here in Switzerland. Recently we went together to Basel to enjoy the city and also to remember that it was the home of our maternal grandmother until she was fifteen and traveled alone to America.

Aunts and uncles, nephews, nieces, cousins. Here, too, we feel a certain responsibility. For Pierre, this sense of responsibility is inherited. Large families in France are closely knit. My family was much smaller and more dispersed. Pierre grew up with family reunions. His grandmother continued her Sunday dinners for the extended family until she was ninety-nine years old. His parents did the same during the long summer vacations. Sometimes I just wanted to be free of the Sunday dinners. When it was our turn to start welcoming home our married children and grandchildren, I remembered the Sunday dinners. We are looking for a middle way, for family reunions that leave room for freedom and spontaneity.

Also our sense of commitment to friends and neighbors. It is a commitment to friendship as well as to specific friends. Together our friends form a universe of connections and journeys and shared stories. We write to one another, now by email. And if we are traveling nearby, we will try to connect and spend some time together. We not only relive memories of our earlier lives but we create new memories. Last spring we reconnected with a colleague and classmate of Pierre's at MIT over forty years ago. We had seen one another once in Paris and another time in Washington. This time we renewed our friendship in Virginia. We shared memories of our days together in Boston, of his wife who died recently, and we promised a visit together the following year in Geneva.

We often see our friends who live close by. Pierre and I both enjoy having company for relaxed informal evenings. Dates are not set long in advance. It is simply a pleasure to be together, to share news, to share our stories, and to share our affection. There is an exchange, there is communion. A coming together, a oneness, the gift of friendship.

We also feel a responsibility to our neighbors, to the community where we live. Let me give an example. As we moved from country to country, in each new setting, we often invited our neighbors for an open house, something that was new wherever we went in Europe. When we arrived in Geneva and moved into a large apartment building, we invited everyone in the building to a housewarming. Our kids put invitations in all the mailboxes. Everyone came. But few followed suit. It took months to break down the barriers, yet slowly it happened. It was easier when we moved to a house. Still today, Pierre and I want to keep our door open for our neighbors.

Housewarming is a good word to describe how we feel about our home, our community, our children's schools, our parish. We start with our home and then our commitment expands in circles—to a community warming, a church warming, a school warming. Where everyone brings their good spirits and together we commit to making the place warm and welcoming.

My maple leaf tugs at my hand. Five lobes suggesting that many commitments: to each other, to our children, to our families, our friends, and our neighbors. And there are many more commitments. Commitment to bringing more beauty into our world, more justice and more love. And I am back to the beginning: commitment to making our marriage work.

JOURNAL PRACTICE 6:
COMMITMENT TO PARENTS

———

Do you remember doing something special, with your partner, for your parents, or for your partner's parents?

- How long ago was it?

- When and where were you?

- Who had the idea?

- How did they react?

- And how did you feel?

- Did it bring you closer to your partner?

- And closer to your parents?

Brenda Ueland continues to encourage us. She promises us that writing is a blessing if we use it. "You will become happier more enlightened, impassioned, and generous to everybody else." She assures us that it is true, we will become happier beings through writing. But to do so we have to write. She reminds us of how long a violinist practices. It is not overnight that a violinist performs at Carnegie Hall. We do not have to try to be soloists. But we do have to learn how to play. And it is only through practice.

⚜ SUGGESTION

There is a well of creative energy within you. Remember that everybody is talented. Your creative talent is in this well. If the well is covered over with worries, distractions, preoccupations, the water will not overflow. Your creativity will not overflow. But if you clear away the muddle, all that is blocking you, the water will overflow. Your creativity will overflow. You will find words for your memories, for your stories.

Remember that writing is a blessing if you do it. You will feel better, happier, more generous to yourself, to your partner, and to those around you.

Find the time and place when and where you are comfortable, take the pen and paper, and write a journal entry about something you and your partner did for your parents or your partner's parents. Enjoy remembering, enjoy writing.

And enjoy sharing. As a happier person, read your writing with your partner or spouse. Share you happiness to be in love.

TAR SPOTS AND COMMITMENT
TO ONESELF

RETURNING TO MY RED MAPLE LEAF, I LOOK NOW AT THE couple of tar spots clustered near the stem. The spots are pitch black. I can remember when I was a little girl trying to scrape them off the leaves. But this only ripped holes in them, sometimes tearing the whole leaf apart. The spots remain. The difficulties between Pierre and me remain. I cannot scrape them away—when we feel that the other does not understand. And still worse, when we feel that the other does not want to understand. Dark spots, not to scratch away, but to recognize. And to deal with as best we can.

Most of these tar spots in our relationship are occasioned by our different temperaments and educations. Pierre is more strict; I'm more lenient. There are daily disagreements, quarrels and, misunderstandings, often harsh and hurtful. Each of us wanting to be right. Each of us being very stubborn. Once after a hateful argument at home, in the late evening, I remember leaving the house and walking for over an hour in the dark. When I finally returned home, Pierre was asleep. This was one of the few times when we went to sleep still angry with the other. We try hard to not let this happen.

We have learned that, if handled with care, the tar spots can sometimes be a good thing, pushing us to new growth and understanding. I can identify one such case that concerned one of our children. Our daughter was anorexic when she was eighteen. It was her first year at college and when she came home for Christmas vacation, she had lost twenty-five pounds. She finished the year but was not well enough to return. I wanted to protect her, to overprotect her. Pierre wanted her to be adult. We argued. Fortunately we also listened to her doctor. We learned to let her be. When she pushed her food aside, we closed our eyes. We helped each other to not interfere but to offer the love our daughter needed. This middle way brought the three of us together. With time she grew stronger, held the anorexia in check. When she fell in love and married, she started to heal.

Our children are now on their own, but this does not mean that we, as parents, always get along with them. The differences still exist. I think of the words about children in *The Prophet* by Kahlil Gibran: "You may give them your love but not your thoughts." This became a mantra for me as the children grew through adolescence. I used to go for walks repeating these words, "You may give them your love. But not your thoughts." This is still difficult. To just listen and, yes, to give them our love. The tar spots still exist.

However, the tar spots do not impact the maple tree's health. Rather they call attention to something within the tree, a life-giving vigor. This is happening. The life-saving sap is starting to flow. And at the same time the dark spots make us appreciate still more the beauty of each red leaf. The beauty of each child and grandchild.

Before leaving these reflections about family, I think about one more commitment that underlies the others: the commitment to oneself. My commitment to myself and Pierre's commitment to himself. Without this underlying commitment, we cannot commit to each other, to our families and friends. I have to be responsible first to myself. To learn to accept the dark spots and cope with them as best I can. I have to tell my over-achieving self to let go, to let others achieve. In the midst of my overactive life, I have to leave space for those following me. Pierre has his own learning to do.

We have each spent time on our own individual development. And we have not shied away from asking for counsel. Pierre did work in transactional analysis. One Christmas a long time ago, when he was in his forties, my mother gave him a copy of *I'm Okay, You're Okay*. It led him to several years of therapy that he deemed both interesting and worthwhile. He recognized the different patterns of behavior on the part of the child, the parent, and the adult, which opened him to new and deeper relationships at home and at work.

I chose to do a Jungian analysis. I called it soul work. It was after the children had left home. I was in my early fifties and returning to my mother tongue, after having raised the children in French. I was also returning to my love of writing. My writing and my foray into Jungian psychology coincided. I chose a Swiss-German analyst here in Geneva, and we worked in French. When I dreamed my first book, *Looking for Gold: A Year in Jungian Analysis*, the dream and my writing were in English. In dealing with the unconscious, there is a common language that makes itself known, no matter the language that we are speaking.

Pierre and I trusted each other as we chose our different paths in our mid-forties and fifties, respectively. And after our years of analysis, we continue on our separate but parallel ways. We share what seems important, we listen carefully to each other. And most importantly, we give each other space. Space to grow. Space to love one another.

As I leave my maple leaf, I know that it will dry, the edges will curl. But next year there will be more leaves. The seasons have taught us trust. The maple trees will again turn bright red. So it is in our relationship. We know that after the long winter and the dark cold nights, spring will come and new leaves will open on the trees. They will stay green all summer. The air will be light and warm. Only then will the leaves turn bright crimson. So it is for our marriage. Winter, spring, summer, autumn. There are seasons also in love. After the storms of springtime, there will be the sunbaths of summer. We are grateful.

JOURNAL PRACTICE 7:
COMMITMENT TO ONESELF

Does the memory of a tar spot, something negative in your relationship, come to mind? If not, skip these questions. Go to the next set, about a bright spot.

Brenda Ueland continues to encourage the writer. "If you once become aware of the richness within you, you will be all right." She promises you that as you discover all the richness within you, you will not only enrich yourself, but also those around you.

- What is your memory of a tar spot?
- What happened?
- Where were you?
- What did you feel?
- How did you cope?
- Has it happened again?

☙ SUGGESTION

Return to your leaf. Imagine a tar spot somewhere on the leaf. Then look again at the rest of the leaf, at the bright green, yellow, or orange. Describe the spot and also the leaf. What colors do your see? Using vivid details brings the experience alive, allowing you to focus on the details rather than the hurt.

Write a short journal entry about the difficulty, the hurt. Then move to the next exercise.

Now find the memory of a bright spot, a positive experience of developing your own self.

- When was it?
- What occasioned it?
- What did you discover?
- Has your commitment been ongoing?
- Were you able to share it with your partner?

✿ SUGGESTION

Let this last journal practice for Commitment feel like a hug for yourself. Sit back and let your words come from the richness within. See the vivid details. Listen to them. Feel them. Describe what sparkles in your memory. And remember that you are talented and original.

Write about a moment of commitment to yourself, when you were taking care of yourself. Enjoy writing about the experience.

Read your one or two short journal entries— the tar spot and the bright spot—to your partner. Share your feeling of being all right. Be all right together.

Go back to the other pages that you wrote in this chapter. Put them together as "Memories of Commitment." And before closing your journal, think about the days ahead. How can you keep these commitments fresh and vibrant? What might you do? Add a postscript to your journal!

Two Sunflowers

CHAPTER THREE

Looking Outward:
Learning from Sunflowers

Geneva, October 12

On my walk this morning, I went up the hillside to the field where sunflowers once looked out over the lake. I write about them in this new chapter. They are now replaced by young vineyards, but I wanted to see them again in my imagination, to feel again how they spread across the field, how their bright yellow faces followed the sun every day.

To remember when the sunflowers stood tall together is to remember when our children stood tall together. Now they are all with their own children. Recently, at our double eightieth birthday celebration, Pierre and I wished each one lasting love. That they continue to stand tall together. That they continue to love one another until they are our age and more.

The comfort I feel in knowing that there is someone close to me, who loves me, is so deep and boundless that I feel a real need to share it. And so this book, with memories of our love story and encouragement to the readers to write memories of their love stories.

I continue to be surprised by the joy and vitality that both Pierre and I feel when we remember together good moments of courtship, of commitment, and now of looking outward. First we remember the moments and then I write about them and read my words to him. We live them twice this way, and still again with each rewrite that I share with Pierre.

In this new chapter I write about how the sunflowers stand side by side with their faces following the sun. Likewise, from the beginning of our marriage, Pierre and I have stood side by side and looked outward. We entered new worlds as we followed our children, our professions, our shared interests. It was like sunshine and rain on the sunflowers.

Today, I want to think about another example from the sunflowers—how when they are mature and fully grown, they no longer turn their faces from east to west each day. Instead, they stay facing toward the east, there where the light rises.

What does this tell me? That Pierre and I no longer need to look in all directions. That we can slow down and stay centered. That we can let go. This will come, maybe not today nor tomorrow, but soon.

And most importantly, for right now, today, it tells me to look in the direction of what I love most. To look at the person I love. To look at Pierre and open my arms to his love.

LOOKING OUTWARD:
FAMILIES AND FRIENDS

I SUGGEST NOW A THIRD STEP TO LASTING LOVE: LOOKING outward. Opening the doors and windows of our relationship to keep it active and flourishing. Antoine de Saint Exupery wrote, "Love is not looking at each other, but looking together in the same direction." Looking together in the same direction.

I think of the sunflowers in the field that used to grow close to our home. When Pierre and I went for walks along the road that borders the field, we were always astonished by the multitude of golden faces standing side by side, looking in the same direction. There were hundreds of them, all standing straight, all facing outward, all following the sun, from east to west.

It is the same in a relationship. Pierre and I look outward together. We cannot live behind closed doors. When we open our doors to go out into the world, we bring the world back with us. When I go for a walk, I come home refreshed. I bring back a few wildflowers and lots of sunshine. Today, when Pierre goes downtown for his work at a humanitarian foundation, he brings back news of different projects to help handicapped children around the world. We go out and when we return home, the world comes with us. There is life, enthusiasm, anticipation.

In writing about sunflowers looking outward, I realize how important it has been for Pierre and me to open the doors and windows of our relationship. From the first months of our marriage until today—fifty-five years—each open door has led us to a new world. Our family was a door, opening into myriad worlds. Other doors were our neighbors and friends. Still another, our professions, taking us to new places and new adventures. As did our pastimes. So many doors to different worlds, all interconnecting.

Memories. Our children taking us by the hand, leading us outward. We looked in their direction like the sunflowers following the sun. We followed them into the worlds of their schools—different schools in different countries—until we settled in Geneva and sent them all to the public lycée at Ferney Voltaire across the border in neighboring France. It was in this new setting that we discovered how politics can enter into the parents' role in the schooling of their children. The one parents' union leaned to the left, and as the French government at that time leaned to the right, there were clashes. We joined in, learning how to lobby for the interests of our children.

Our kids led us also into their worlds of sports—swimming, skiing, and soccer. Summer days I drove them to the village pools in Grand Lancy—four pools with a wonderful canal from the dressing room to the intermediate pool. In winter we skied close by, either in the Jura Mountains or the Alps. The ski slopes on the Jura side were so close that our oldest son would go on his moped with the skis attached to his backpack. Soccer was a new experience for us, a new sport and a new setting. Pierre went the most often to watch our youngest son, while I drove the girls to ballet lessons. Our youngest daughter continued to dance in a program at the Grand Théâtre. We went to all the different performances and then waited for her at the backstage door. Still another world.

It was especially our love of music that opened wide the doors of our family. Each of our children played the piano; it was part of our family life—sharing the piano bench. Twenty minutes each, Czerny, Bach, Mozart. Mozart, Bach, Czerny. How many times did we sit with other parents awaiting our children's performance at the yearly recitals? It took us back to our own childhoods, to the years of music lessons I had and to the ones that Pierre wished he hadn't stopped. We wanted to give this experience to our children. And now they are giving it to their children. We listen to our grandkids play the piano and we remember.

Schools, sports, music, looking outward through our children. There were other doors. As they were growing through their teens, there was also the world of parties and nights out. Confronting their wishes for later, longer hours, more freedom, fewer controls. Comparing notes with other parents, deciding together when to ease up on the rules and when to hold on to them. I remember the first *boom*—the French word for a dance party—that we had at our house. It was for our oldest son's birthday, he was fifteen. He and his friends, girls and boys, played volleyball outside, then went down to the playroom in the basement to dance. He claims we sent everyone home at ten o'clock. A year and a half later, another party, this time his sister's fifteenth birthday. She invited a dozen classmates including her steady boyfriend. They skipped the volleyball outside and went right to the basement room to dance. When we realized there was no more noise from downstairs, we went to see if all was well. The lights were turned off. We turned them back on, went back upstairs, and waited until midnight to usher everyone out.

It was good to be two, to talk through how we should react, what we should do, what we should not do. And the questions grew more difficult as the children grew older. There were sleepovers and requests to come home very late, or simply to stay out all night. We were letting go of more of our rules. The kids were encouraging us, and we were trusting them.

Happily there are also grandchildren to lead us outward. Little bundles of energy who see the world with fresh eyes, who wake up content each morning, who help us do the same. Our hearts open when they come for a visit, sometimes for an overnight. Pierre and I watch them play with the same Legos® our kids played with, but they build sky ships and space stations instead of trains and railroad tracks. They read the same books, the old Tintin ones, Scotch-taped, with loose pages. Now the youngest ones are nine and ten. They still read Tintin, but electronic games have replaced the Legos.

Recently we went to listen to our Geneva-based grandchildren in their end-of-the-year concert. Visiting the school, waiting in the courtyard with other parents and other children, then sitting together in the large auditorium gave us a glimpse into today's public schools in Geneva. First, we watched the younger grandson, eleven years old, and his class take their places and sing a full half hour of songs, all learned by heart. Then there was the older granddaughter, thirteen years old, and a longer program of songs.

We remembered doing the same thing for our grandson in Brooklyn at a spring concert at his school. Our grandson plays the trumpet. There were about eight young boys and girls playing the trumpet. Amazing to watch them all standing straight, all about the same height, and all holding their trumpets high into the air. In both settings, it was heartening to see our grandkids so happy to perform and so stimulated.

Our older grandkids send us occasional emails and text messages and sometimes come by for a short visit. Sometimes they ask for help on a school paper in English. I willingly offer, even if I don't always understand the subject. Sometimes they share with us a difficult relationship, a missed opportunity, a dashed hope. They are already another generation of sunflowers. They keep us on our toes with their different computer programs, their iPads and iPhones. Three summers ago, I decided the best way to keep up with them was to buy an iPhone myself. My fifteen year old grandson answered all my questions, not just patiently explaining how to do something, but making me hold the phone and do it myself. A smart teacher.

Our friends also take us into new worlds. In fact they take us in all directions. There was our first babysitter in Brussels, a foreign student from Tunisia, who invited us to his small hotel on Djerba for our twenty-fifth wedding anniversary; there are the friends in New Orleans who invited us to their home one spring for the annual Jazz Festival. We are fortunate to live in Geneva, such an international city, where we easily meet expats working here at the United Nations. And then there's the Geneva Writers' Group, the association of writers that I started with a few friends twenty years ago, where we now have friends of all nationalities.

I think of an Afghan poet whose poems in Farsi have been published and who is now writing in English. He left Afghanistan when the Russians were fighting the Taliban. His wife is Pakistani, working for the United Nations here in Geneva. He is a stay-at-home father, working on a second novel. His first novel relates the story of two brothers growing up in Afghanistan during the rise of the Taliban and the Russian and American wars, and how they choose different paths. There is also an Iraqi who sought political asylum in Switzerland several years back. He is writing his own story in English, how he was kidnapped while working on the side of the West during the second Iraq war. These are new worlds that we are discovering.

We cherish both new friendships and older ones—including people from our school years and from the countries where we once lived. We keep track of our old friends, we go to them, they come to us. I think of an American family we met when their four sons and our three daughters were together for a semester at the lycée at Ferney Voltaire. The father was on a sabbatical at CERN, the high-energy research center in Geneva.

We parents hoped that some of the friendships and flirtations might develop into lasting relationships, but they all went their different ways. However, we adults stayed close and continue to see one another every year, in the States or here.

As we reach out to family and friends, there is fresh air, cross ventilation. We learn the lesson of the sunflowers. We stand side by side looking in the same direction and sharing the love that is ours.

JOURNAL PRACTICE 8:
FAMILY AND FRIENDS

Do you have a memory of doing something with one of your children or one of your friends that took you outward, that opened a door to a new world?

- Where did you go?
- What do you remember of the setting?
- What was the weather?
- Were you happy to go?
- Was there fresh air, excitement?
- Did you discover something new?
- How long ago was it?
- Would you wish to do it again?

Listen to another writing teacher, William Zinsser. In his book On Writing Well, *he counsels us to write about what we have experienced. "Of all the subjects available to you as a writer, the one you know best is yourself." We should write about ourselves, and we should do so in simple language. Zinsser warns against unnecessary words, pompous frills, useless jargon. "Fighting clutter is like fighting weeds." Simplify, simplify, he insists.*

⁂ SUGGESTION
You are writing about yourself—a subject you know well. You do not need to explain, to digress, to find excuses.

Simplify what you are writing. Avoid long words, complicated words, unnecessary words. As you remove all the muddle blocking your well of creativity, also remove all the clutter blocking your writing. Write without second thoughts. Let your words flow. Think of the sunflowers. One memory. One flower on each stem.

Write a new journal entry, the date, and the place. Describe the setting. Write slowly to see the colors. To remember how you felt. Just one or two paragraphs.

Look for the opportunity to share this new page in your love story with your spouse or partner. Do they remember the same event? Do they remember another experience with a child or a friend, another open door to the outside world?

LOOKING OUTWARD: PROFESSIONS

Pierre and I looked outward also through our professions. I remember my sunflowers—each standing tall and yet no one flower overshadowing another. In our relationship, it was Pierre's profession that gave us the means to raise a large family. But we stood tall together, Pierre mostly outside the house and me mostly inside. It was during an era when women were expected to stay home and men were the wage earners. It was not always an easy choice, if indeed it was a choice.

I remember well when I was sometimes too busy with the children at home, I would ask Pierre to bring the world home with him in the evening, to tell me what was going on in his office, what was happening outside our home. "Tell me about the people you saw today. What were they talking about?" I felt numbed, talking all day long with kids under ten and reading *Oui-Oui* books by Enid Blyton in French. And the busy years continued.

Pierre's profession took us from France, to Belgium, to Italy, to the States, to Switzerland, each time opening up a new world—a new setting, new culture, and sometimes a new language. So many memories of different countries. First in France where Pierre was doing his military service, two and a half years in the Air Force. It was during the Algerian war. We were together in Provence, at an airbase in the small village of Istres. It was my apprenticeship in becoming a French housewife. The closest American in the area was the wife of the Communist mayor of Arles, an hour away. I never met her.

From there we moved to Brussels where Pierre worked at the Common Market—the early European Union grouping together France, Belgium, Luxembourg, Holland, Germany, and Italy. Europe was becoming a reality. The children would go to European schools. There were plans and hopes for a common passport, a common currency. Skeptics called us dreamers.

Next Pierre was sent to a research center at Ispra, on Lago Maggiore in northern Italy. We lived up a narrow road on a hillside without a telephone. When I needed to call the doctor, I had to run down the hill to the public telephone in the village bistro. The doctor couldn't believe that we lived on a hillside with four kids without a phone.

Then came a year in the States—Pierre at MIT. Living in my country was not always easy for us. Pierre reacted negatively to certain things that I took for granted, like respecting signs or waiting one's turn at the post office. Sometimes I understood but other times I was not happy with his quite typical French reaction. It was then time for an overdue monthly date, to help us find a middle ground.

We were slowly realizing that, as a bicultural couple, we did better living in a neutral country. In the States, Pierre was tempted to blame me for whatever got on his nerves. And similarly, in France I was tempted to blame Pierre for whatever got on my nerves.

So it was that we arrived in neutral Switzerland where Pierre accepted a job for an American computer company, opening its headquarters in Geneva. Housing was scarce, and we quickly discovered that in the city of Calvin there were very few large families. We also learned that children were expected to be quiet and behave. With training and time, ours learned to walk in line, even on the sidewalk.

Outside the home, Pierre was calling the shots. I was calling them inside the home. There was a division of work and of decision-making. In retrospect, it was our sharing each month, our monthly dates, that helped us manage our everyday busy lives. If I wasn't happy with Pierre coming home late, we'd change the daily routine to make life easier for both of us. If Pierre felt he didn't have time to play with the kids, we'd free up the weekends for happy time. The few notes I took during our monthly dates—yes, I made notes—let us keep track of whether or not we were finding answers that worked.

When the older children left for university, the rhythm changed. I found time to return to my mother tongue and to writing. Another door opened. I reached out to English-language writers living in Geneva and soon to writers living in the States. I joined different writers' associations, attended readings and conferences, and found journals and magazines, and soon publishers, for my work. I was entering a whole new world.

A few years later I started to teach creative writing both in Geneva and in the States. Most of the time, Pierre and I would travel to the States together for the workshops and readings I was giving. From the east across to the west, to cities and parts of American where I had never been. Doors opened wide for the two of us.

Here at home where I teach each month for the Geneva Writers' Group, Pierre comes with me to the Press Club to welcome the writers for a Saturday of writing. He claims that he is our professional coffee maker. Occasionally he stays to write and to join us for a sandwich at lunchtime. It is a world we share that continues to flourish.

For the last years of his professional life, Pierre returned to work in Brussels for the European Commission which had grown to include fifteen member countries. I stayed in Geneva, writing and teaching. We saw one another on weekends. The waiting and anticipation of seeing one another added an element of new romance to our relationship.

Since Pierre's retirement, it has become an Indian summer in our marriage. We have more time, we enjoy our lives at home and continue to find new energy in looking outward. I with my writing and teaching, and Pierre with his work at the Geneva-based foundation. We both are stimulated with new interests and thoughts. And each of us is grateful to have someone ready and happy to listen.

Although our worlds continue to expand, worlds sometimes seem to grow smaller for many people in their seventies. But this can signal adventure: an unexplored domain, waiting for new initiatives, new programs—ways to keep elders active and involved in our communities. How can we keep enlarging our horizons? How can we keep looking outward to the world around us?

JOURNAL PRACTICE 9: PROFESSIONS

Find an experience of looking outward through your profession, your work, that acted like a tonic when you shared it with your partner

- What were you doing?
- Were there other people involved?
- Was there a challenge?
- And then satisfaction?
- Do you remember what was said?
- Was it a one-time happening?
- Were you happy to share it with your partner?

Zinsser says, "Give yourself permission to write about yourself and have a good time doing it." Give yourself permission. Ego is healthy. It's egotism that is a pain. So relax and enjoy writing. Write as if you are talking to someone else on paper. If you enjoy writing your story, writes Zinsser, chances are the writing will be good. You will find your own voice. It's your story. And chances are that the reader will enjoy it.

🎋 SUGGESTION

Journals are capacious, like our writing desks. They can include personal notes, anecdotes, reflections, conversations, photos, drawings, even lists. To bring the story of your experience alive, try including a few lines of dialogue. Don't worry about remembering word for word what was said. Remember rather the gist and the tone of the conversation. A bit of dialogue brightens the page. Gives life to your journal entry.

Remember the sunflowers. Each flower bright and alive. Each flower facing the sun.

Sit back and enjoy writing for ten minutes. Relate the experience. No extra words. Maybe read what you have written. Underline something that made you smile. Something that you enjoyed.

Let yourself relive the new energy that looking outward brought to you and to your relationship. Share the memory with your partner or spouse.

LOOKING OUTWARD:
SHARED INTERESTS

FAMILIES, FRIENDS, PROFESSIONS—ALL DIFFERENT windows through which to look outward. There are also the shared interests that Pierre and I pursue that widen our horizons and nourish our relationship. Reading, music, art, cinema, sports, and more. Pierre reads more novels and books about history, I read more memoirs and books about spirituality. This lets us learn from one another and share the worlds we enter with each new book.

At breakfast, often we bring something we read the night before. I'll bring a few lines from Thomas Merton, whose books I continue to read and reread. This winter I went back to *Zen and the Birds of Appetite.* I remember reading something about Zen getting us back to the direct experience of life, "without logical verbalizing." When I read that to Pierre, the "logical verbalizing" made us laugh. How often I chide him for being too rational and he chides me for being irrational. We've examined Jung's four types of personality, and we are pretty much direct opposites: Pierre is first a thinking type; I am first an intuiting type. The challenges inherent in this have been good for us.

Not long ago, Pierre was reading about the crusades. He shared an article about Saint Francis of Assisi going along on the fifth crusade, unarmed, wanting to discuss his faith with the Sultan of Egypt. The Sultan accepted. They met and discussed their different faiths. Afterwards, Francis tried to insert in his Rule the necessity of listening to the defenders of other faiths—in particular of Islam. He was refused the imprimatur by the Pope. People tried to open doors; others sought to keep them closed. Our discussion opened our minds to the disasters and tragedies one's faith can unfortunately lead to.

Sometimes we read the same book together. For instance, Barack Obama's *Dreams from My Father*. Besides appreciating the author and his style of writing, we appreciated learning about life in Indonesia, in Kenya, and also of community organizing in Chicago. I remember a passage describing when Obama's father visits him, the one time, in Honolulu. The young Obama is ten years old, living in his grandparents' house. Just before leaving, his father unearthed two records in dull brown dust jackets. "Barry! Look here—I forgot that I had brought these for you. The sounds of your continent." And soon his father was dancing, his arms swaying, casting an invisible net over him. The phenomenon of belonging to two worlds. Pierre and I talked deeply about this. My two worlds are closer than Obama's but still they pull me in different directions.

Another interest directing our attention outward is music. After all the lessons that our children took, it is now Pierre taking piano lessons from our son who teaches at the Conservatory in Fribourg. Pierre goes once a month by train—a beautiful ride along the lake, then up into the foothills of the Alps—for his lesson and stays for lunch. Time for father and son over the piano and the lunch table. When he practices at home, I again hear Czerny, Bach, Mozart—twenty minutes, but just one rendition—evoking memories of children playing the piano, one after another.

And there are also our grandchildren. Almost all of them play the piano. We listen to them when we visit in their homes—in Brooklyn, Paris, Geneva or Fribourg. It's as if our piano bench has been cloned. And when they come to us, it's concert time. They learn to take their turns like their parents did.

Sometimes we just enjoy listening to recordings at home, appreciating a symphony, a concerto. I have mentioned dancing to Paganini. The recording is "Six Sonatas for Violin and Guitar." We have only to hear a few chords and we're on our feet. Another favorite recording is the concert Vladimir Horowitz gave in Moscow on his first return to Russia in 1986. As we listen to Scarlatti and Mozart and Rachmaninoff, the response of the audience grows in thunderous applause and we get caught up in the emotion his music created. Our senses are awakened.

It's the same when we go to a painting exhibit and we take time to look at a collection of Monet, of Chagall, of Modigliani. Recently, while visiting Pierre's youngest brother in southern France, we climbed to the bluff at Aix-en-Province where Cezanne painted his many views of the spectacular Mont

Sainte-Victoire. On top of the hill, there was an exhibit of a dozen reproductions of his paintings, illustrating their progression, how each painting became less and less figurative, and how Cezanne became one of the founders of modern art. We were given a lesson in perception. The shared experience heightened not only our emotional response to the mountain and the paintings, but it heightened our physical response to each other. Beauty aroused a sensation and invited sharing.

Likewise when we go to the theater or to the cinema. When we take the person we love out in the evening, to see a play, a movie, there is courtship. A date in Geneva, a glimpse of the nightlife. Parking under the lake and walking across the streets, glittering with lights and people and motion. Or watching a video at home. Just the two of us. We make ourselves comfortable and enjoy a good film, even if our screen is not large. We stay up-to-date with the current cinematic and theatrical culture and can share our impressions with our children and friends. Our imaginations are kindled by the arts.

There is also the world of sports that beckons to us. For years Pierre and I played tennis together—including going away to a tennis camp for a week—until I hurt my shoulder and he had to find another partner. But the sport continues to draw our attention. We watch the different tournaments on TV, cheering for Federer the Swiss champion—again revealing our wish to remain neutral, to let the French and American players work it out themselves. And this past spring, we particularly followed

Roland Garros, looking for our fifteen-year-old grandson who was a ball catcher. He told us that each morning at 6 a.m., they were out running to be in shape for the day's match.

Until recently, we continued to ski together. Living in Geneva, we are spoiled by the proximity of the Alps. We knew by heart the ski station of Samoëns, just an hour from our house, where Pierre's family has a large chalet. The station has a family rate for people like us. But as the children started to leave home, or to go skiing on their own, Pierre and I started to discover the different ski stations farther away, around Switzerland. A favorite memory is our first weekend at Zermatt. We left Geneva early in the morning on a Friday. By early afternoon we were at the top of Zermatt, at 3,000 meters, on a glacier, bright blue sky, freezing weather, foreheads pounding from the altitude, but completely exhilarated to be at the top of the world.

We have tried to share our happiness in small ways with those around us. With our children and their families. With neighbors and friends. So many people are living alone without the love and support of a spouse. When we wake up in the morning, we know there is someone at our side who loves us. Pierre and I wish to bring the warmth of these moments to those who are less fortunate. A phone call, a visit, an invitation. It takes but a moment.

We try to find ways to do this, through our schools and churches, through our community organizations, through our political affiliations. Even voting directs an outward effort, which can be time-consuming—every two months in the "hands-on" democracy of Switzerland. If citizens can muster up enough signatures, they can initiate referendums. When we both became Swiss, we kept our native nationalities. So Pierre also votes in France, and I—by correspondence—in New York.

We want to contribute to making the world a more peaceful place for our children and grandchildren, for all children and grandchildren. Utopia perhaps. But we know that in making the world safer for just one child, we are contributing to making it safer for all children. We trust the butterfly effect—where the flap of a butterfly's wings in Brazil can set off a tornado in Japan. Where a small change in one place of the world can result in a large change in another place. Where something we do wherever we are living will have a ripple effect, touching people in ever widening circles—like when we toss a pebble into a pond and watch the concentric circles, rippling always more outward. It's the peace that we create around us that will contribute to the peace of the world for our grandchildren.

I return to my sunflowers. When they are full-grown, they no longer turn their heads to follow the sun. Instead they face eastward all day. They face where the light will rise each morning. Their example is a lesson for Pierre and me. In this Indian summer of our lives, now that we are "full-grown," we are learning to look to where we can best continue to serve and to love.

JOURNAL PRACTICE 10:
SHARED INTERESTS

What memory of a shared interest comes to you, an experience that widened the way you see the world?

- How did it happen?
- What caught your attention?
- What especially interested you?
- Did it interest your partner?
- Did you talk about it?
- What did you say?
- Would you wish to experience it again?

Zinsser reminds us that it is in writing that we discover what we have to offer. With each page of writing, we discover something more about ourselves. We learn what is important for us. "One of the best gifts you have to offer when you write personal history is the gift of yourself." Think of what you are putting on paper. The gift of yourself to your partner, to your reader.

❧ SUGGESTION

Let your journal entry be a gift of yourself. Remember there are no rules. You are writing freely, relating a memory, reliving an experience. Seeing it anew. Feeling it anew. Touching anew. You are writing about yourself. You can reveal your quirks and shortcomings as well as your skills and talents. Likewise, it is

in writing about your partner that you will get to know him or
her better. His or her quirks and skills and interests. What are
your best selves? Keep discovering them through writing.

*Write your journal entry slowly. Write about yourself and your
partner looking outward. And maybe draw a sunflower. It
doesn't have to be a copy of Van Gogh's sunflower. Rather your
sunflower. Draw two sunflowers, side by side.*

*Put your three last pages together as "Memories of Looking
Outward." Then find when it's the right moment to open your
pages to your partner. Maybe he or she has different memories.
What does looking outward evoke for the two of you? In sharing
your memories, you are sharing yourself. Your pages are a gift of
yourself to your loved one. Love notes.*

Sea Glass

CHAPTER FOUR

Looking Inward:
The Glow of Sea Glass

Geneva, October 14

Yesterday morning, instead of writing a journal entry, I turned to my emails and was submerged. The day disappeared. Waves of messages—tugging at me, asking for attention, asking for reflection, asking to be answered.

Now it is already late in the afternoon and I am only beginning journal entry number four to introduce this new chapter and to write about pieces of sea glass. When will I learn to write first and then turn to my mail!? I will keep trying.

Back to my sea glass, I grew up without knowing about sea glass. We lived inland from the ocean. It was only fairly recently, about ten years ago, that I came upon pieces of sea glass on a small solitary beach on Cranberry Island off the coast of Maine. I was alone, Pierre was sailing. I was looking for shells, Instead I found pieces of sea glass—pink, light blue, soft green, a tangerine yellow. The pieces nestled tight in the wet sand, as if holding on, not wanting to be pulled back into the sea. I picked them up, one piece after another, always finding still more.

As I washed off the sand, the pieces glowed in my hand. I remember holding them up to the sunlight, and seeing how they seemed to glimmer both from without and from within. They were magical, each one with a story of its own. How long had they been tossed about in the ocean, rubbed against the rocky depths before being deposited on the beach at Cranberry Island?

The pieces are now in a crystal vase in our bedroom. I have just picked out two of them. One is light green, the other is tangerine, both have been rubbed soft by the surf. I put them on the wooden lamp stand on top of my desk. They make me think of Pierre and me. The green one is larger, sturdier, shaped like a tree. The tangerine one is smaller and rounder, its edges like petals. It could be a simple flower. The colors complement one another, and the shapes go side by side.

I will keep the two sea glass pieces on my desk. They will remind me that Pierre and I are like pieces of sea glass, embedded on the beach and, when held up to the light, we wish to glimmer both from within and from without.

As I end this journal entry, I remember that in the beginning I wrote about the waves of emails tugging at me, asking to be answered. The sea glass tells me to nestle into my writing. To not be pulled out to sea by the waves.

FINDING THE SPARK WITHIN

GOD TELLS THE PROPHET EZEKIEL, "I AM ABOUT TO kindle a fire in you." It is in looking inward that I discover this fire. I turn to sea glass, an image that will lead me to memories of looking inward. I have a collection of sea glass that I collected on the Atlantic Coast.

Sea glass becomes beautiful only after rolling in the sand and surf. First it is a fragment of colored glass from a broken bottle, rough and jagged. With the scuffing of waves, it is sanded and shaped into something smooth to touch. When I hold it in the light, it glows. I like to think there is a spark inside the piece of glass which, with the movement of the ocean currents, begins to glimmer, illuminating the glass from within. And I like to think it is so in lasting love. There is a spark within each of us that, with care and attention, starts to shine, so that not only do Pierre and I begin to faintly glimmer, but so does our relationship.

All of us know certain couples who warm our hearts. We want to be near them, to stay in their company. They radiate calm and contentment. They are like lighthouses perched on the shores of humanity, offering safety and hospitality. I think of Baucis and Philemon in Ovid's *Metamorphoses* who welcomed two dusty wayfarers to their humble dwelling, sharing what little they had—mottled berry, wild cherries, radishes, a piece of cheese, and eggs—not knowing that the two visitors were disguised gods who have come down to earth looking for human goodness.

The gods, Jupiter and Mercury, had gone to a thousand homes looking for somewhere to rest and found the thousand homes bolted and barred against them. Only one house opened its doors, the home of a good-hearted old woman and her loving husband. The Gods decided to inundate the entire land in retribution, except for the humble cottage of Baucis and Philemon. Before going on their way, the two dusty wayfarers granted their hosts whatever wish they chose. Baucis and Philemon asked to never be separated. "Since we have lived so long together, let neither of us ever have to live alone. Grant that we may die together." Their wish was granted. When they died, they became two trees growing close to one another, the linden and the oak, nourishing one another, offering shade and shelter together. From far and wide people came to hang wreaths of flowers on their branches in honor of the faithful couple.

Baucis and Philemon learned in their long years together to withstand whatever hardships came their way. "We are poor folk," Baucis said to her unidentified visitors, "but poverty isn't so bad when you're willing to own up to it, and a contented spirit is a great help, too." Together Baucis and her loving husband Philemon found the way to live with a contented spirit. This is the lesson that I draw from their story: for lasting love, Pierre and I must nourish a contented spirit.

This is also the lesson that I draw from the pieces of sea glass that I collected late one summer day along the shores of

Cranberry Island. Pierre and I were visiting friends from our university days. Everyone else was out sailing. I was alone, walking along the beach at sunset when I came upon pieces of sea glass and took several with me. Baucis and Philemon lived with very little, but with "a contented spirit." My pieces of sea glass tell me that this contented spirit is within, that it is what makes the sea glass glow, just as it made Baucis and Philemon glow. To nourish my own glow, I must look inward.

Pierre and I were led to look inward very soon after we first met by the death of his younger sister during our year together at the University of Grenoble. Christine was my age, twenty-two, and was dying from a rare lung cancer. The very night of her death, another friend and I drove Pierre to his home when the car skidded off the road in a blinding ice and snowstorm. It was close to midnight. We walked to the nearest village to find a telephone. Pierre's father came to take us to their house for the night. Christine had died just hours earlier upstairs in her bedroom.

During the rest of that long night and the next morning, I witnessed the faith of his family as they kept vigil. And as they welcomed me into their home in the midst of their deep grief. I was afraid of death and had had no experience of it. All night I listened to their steps on the wooden staircase going up to her room, coming down from her room. Her parents, Pierre, and his seven younger brothers, his one older sister. The night was my wrestling with the angel, like Jacob. My wanting to believe what I perceived they believed. That death was not the end. That somehow life—in a very deep sense—continued.

In the morning, the storm had passed. Fresh snow covered the front yard, the hedges, the low fruit trees to the left, the tall pine trees to the right. Everything sparkled under the blue sky. I joined Pierre's family for breakfast, nine children and two parents sitting around the large dining table, making room for an American.

Back at Grenoble, Pierre and I sought out each other's company to talk about his sister's death. We asked ourselves questions that often we brush aside, especially when we are young. Why was it Christine, someone so young? Where was God when she was dying? Where was she now? This honest sharing, and deep searching for truth, laid the foundation for our growing friendship. Neither of us was trying to impress the other. We were questioning ourselves and looking for meaning in Christine's death. We were learning to trust each other, to listen carefully to our differences and to share our thoughts and hopes.

This experience was an important step along my way to entering the Catholic Church. During my three years of boarding school, I appreciated the chapel services and the liturgy of the Anglican Church which fed my imaginative soul more than the Sunday services of the Congregational Church of my childhood. At university, studying literature and philosophy, I continued to be drawn to a more mystical faith. When I went to do graduate study in France, I wanted to learn more about the Catholic Church. I did not imagine that the death of a girl my age would leave its permanent mark upon me, as did the Angel wrestling with Jacob in the Old Testament, leading me to embrace the faith of her family.

Another memory, one year later, the summer before our marriage, when a Dominican priest, Father Kaelin, welcomed me into the Catholic Church. I had returned to France to see if I felt ready to enter the Catholic Church and to learn if I felt ready to envisage my life in France, side by side with Pierre. It was a quiet ceremony in the ancient church of Samoëns in the French Alps. It was raining. Clouds did not open, bells did not ring. But the centuries of prayer accumulated in the ancient stone walls held me in their clasp. Pierre and his parents were with me. My parents in New York were in my heart. We all believed in the same one God.

Today I still learn from my pieces of sea glass. They share their stories, of plummeting into the sea, of shipwrecks, of riptides and whirlpools. I have offered pieces from my collection of sea glass to my writing classes, asking the participants to write from the sea glass they hold in their hand. The stories have astonished me—how these small pieces of sea glass are able to call up memories of lost parents, of happy or sad childhoods, of love affairs. I still have a handful—pale pink, green, yellow, light blue—in a glass vase in our bedroom. They remind me to hold on to my inner beliefs. Beliefs that ground us, letting us stand firm and keep our heads above the waves, letting us glow from within.

During the many years of our long life together, Pierre and I have continued to believe that within the human heart there is goodness, there is compassion, there is a longing for

SUSAN M. TIBERGHIEN

justice. We know of so many people in different places around the world who are giving of themselves to improve the lot of others. We think of the stories of the young people who come to the foundation where Pierre works to ask for funding for their projects in underdeveloped countries, young people who are giving several years of their lives to making life easier for others. We wish that their inspiring stories would be known and shared, that these stories would be printed in the press rather than the violent stories of crime and war.

Going back to memories of the early years of our marriage, after Pierre's military service in southern France, I remember when we were living in Brussels. Our second child was born there shortly after our arrival. Pierre was working to make the dream of a united Europe a reality. It was the time of the Second Vatican Council. Pope John XXIII was opening the doors of the Vatican to a more tolerant ecumenical church. We were again participating in a group of young couples looking for ways to live our faith as married Christians. We met once a month at one of the couples' homes, bringing our hopes and our deceptions, our questions and our answers. Listening to how other couples were handling their lives, their children, and their spirituality helped us talk through our own ideas and beliefs.

It was in Brussels that we discovered an Orthodox monastery in the Ardennes where we both appreciated the moving liturgy and the chants of the monks. Even our young children were captivated by the drama of the liturgy, the flickering lights, the movement of the priest, the incensement of the icons.

They sat on mats on the stone floor for the long services, we stood behind them, participating as it were in the service.

In whatever church we worshipped, we returned often to one of our favorite passages from the Gospel of John, where Jesus encounters the Samaritan woman at the well and asks for a drink of water. He instructs her that "God is spirit. And those who worship must worship in spirit and truth." This was the God that Pierre and I wanted to worship.

At home, we wanted to open the minds and worlds of our children to include the people around us, to give them a solid ground of trust. I have warm memories of a foreign student who was in an English class I was teaching. He was from Chad— tall, good-looking, dark with tribal marks on his cheeks. He came often to our home and thrilled our kids by dancing to a Bellefonte record as they clapped their hands to the rhythm. We have stayed in touch with him and his Chadian wife. He came back to visit us while we were living in Italy. When we went for walks, people often turned around to stare at this tall handsome African holding the hands of our young children. He shared his Animist faith with us, helping us to expand our own beliefs and to see the presence of God in all the creation.

Our monthly couple dates offered us a way to stay on track. We usually looked forward to these dates. We were careful to listen to each other, to take the time to appreciate both our differences and our togetherness. But when we were angry with one another, we would instead look for reasons to postpone the next date. Fortunately the dates were in place on our calendars, and they served us well, teaching us to put on hold some of our arguments while waiting for a quieter moment. They gave us a bit of distance and a clearer perspective.

Still today the monthly dates serve us well. We look at where we are in our relationship, in our own spiritual lives. We learn from the lesson of the sea glass that glowed on the beach at Cranberry Island We nourish the spark within each of us so that together we nourish our marriage.

JOURNAL PRACTICE 11:
THE SPARK WITHIN

Were there times when you questioned one another about your beliefs, your faith? Was there an experience that brought you together on a spiritual level?

- What occasioned the exchange?
- Was it a sunset, an expanse of countryside, waves in the ocean?
- Were you caught in a moment of awe?
- Were you silent?
- Or did you find words to express your wonder?
- Did you reach out to your partner?
- Has it happened again?

Dorothea Brande, in her introduction to her acclaimed Becoming a Writer, *writes "This book is all about the writer's magic." And she proceeds to show the reader how writing opens a way to a more creative life. "Turn yourself gently, in a relaxed and pleasant frame of mind, in the direction you want to go." Turn yourself gently toward your pages. The inner voice will find its way to your page because writing is magic.*

♣ SUGGESTION

Turn yourself gently toward your writing. Look for images that open the way. It's the images in our writing that release our emotions. In journal writing, we go within, we find an experience that we want to write about, or the experience finds us. We start to describe it, and we come upon an image. Something we can see, perhaps in the setting, the late afternoon sunlight, or in the description of the person we are with, maybe her eyes or his open hands. We pause, we hold on to the image. It awakens an emotion. We relive the moment. All this in a journal entry.

Think about the pieces of sea glass that sparkle in the sunlight. The image of sea glass.

Breathe deeply and start a new journal entry. Move into the memory, turn yourself gently to it. Write slowly. If you come upon an image, stop for a moment. Let it take you deeper.

Then look for the time to share your memory and writing with your partner. Let him or her feel your emotion. Experience together the magic of writing.

FACING STORMS AND DARKNESS

In a long relationship, the storms keep coming. The pieces of sea glass keep tumbling in the surf. When we were young, we did not imagine the power of the currents ahead of us. We saw ourselves swimming over the waves, enjoying the sun on our backs. But there are rollers and breakers, and with each new one the relationship is rocked about. As the children were growing up, it was pretty much little children, little problems. We thought we were handling both pretty well. There were temper tantrums and fights—usually between the same two or three of them. There were close calls with illnesses and accidents. But the children recovered and so did we. Or so we thought. We did not know that one of our daughters was being pulled down by an undertow we could not imagine. I will write about this shortly. For now, I continue remembering as it was then.

There were difficult adolescent years for our children—times when they refused to speak to us, when they did not come home at night, when they threatened to do something foolish and dangerous. We needed our monthly dates to talk through how best to handle these bigger difficulties, how to come to an agreement about our position. Both of us vividly remember a phone call from the police at two o'clock in the morning. One of our children had been arrested for breaking into the private yachts and boats at the harbor. We were called to identify him. We drove into town not knowing what to expect. Furious boat owners awaited us, as did the police. Our son did not want to look at us. We shared our broken hearts and looked for ways to mend, to get back on track with one another.

Memories of how we struggled with the drinking and drugs. There were a few terrible years at the lycée when drug dealers were crossing the border from Geneva to hook naïve students in France. For some of our children, it was a sort of initiation. For others it was more dangerous. Clans formed and members were sworn to secrecy. A resulting tragic death created shock waves. At first we tried to interfere. We learned that discussion and trust were more effective than punishment.

We tried to identify the values that we deemed essential to the wellbeing of our children, but we felt tossed about and pulled in different directions. We turned to family therapy for help during a dark, difficult period of adolescence for one of our children. The sessions were monthly. Pierre and I, our teenager, his counselor, and the psychiatrist sat at a round table. Tempers flared. Fists hit the walls. Tears flowed. I remember our son finally standing up and leaving the room. Pierre and I followed him. It was the turning point.

We faced also our own storms. I went through a couple of years feeling alone and forsaken with the six children to take care of and a husband who was often absent, away on business trips. I wanted to "go home." My thoughts went back to Briarcliff Manor and my parents, and I felt that they were my home. On the other side of the ocean. I blamed my difficulties on France where we were then living, where the children were at the lycée. It all seemed foreign. Each new wave pushed me deeper down.

Pierre had his own crescendo breakers. Afraid of losing his job, and with a wife and six children to support, he worked harder and harder. There was no room for time off. No time to think about his wife. No time to think about his children. Finally he was transferred to another department. He caught his breath. And I caught mine. It was about then that we went away for our weekend, to the hotel in the Drôme that I wrote about in the chapter on courtship, where we warmed ourselves in front of the large wood fire and sipped the sweet Muscat wine. We relaxed and listened to one another. And we loved one another all over again.

It was still later when Pierre and I were in our mid-sixties, that an even more powerful, a horrendous breaker hit us. Our middle daughter revealed that she had been abused by one of our parish priests when she was eight years old. The priest was giving her "private" lessons to help her prepare for her first communion. She had buried the experience deep in her unconscious. The memories of abuse were awakened when her own son at the same age, eight years old, was preparing for his first communion. She was then thirty-six years old.

We had let our daughter be abused, injured most intimately, one afternoon each week for a month. At the first communion, we had watched as the priest held her hand walking down the aisle of the church, followed by the other children. Our daughter had said nothing. Until twenty-eight years later when she said, "You should have known." We did not know. As our daughter accused us of not protecting her, Pierre and I turned to each other. Why had we not seen anything? How had I, who had chosen to be a stay-at-home mom, not seen something? How had Pierre become so busy in his profession that he was often not there for his children? We told each other our fears and our misgivings. We tried to uncover and acknowledge all that we had not done for her.

And we listened to our daughter. For six years we stood with her husband at her side, as she asked for justice. And with the Swiss Dominican priest, Father Kaelin, the priest who had welcomed me into the church fifty years earlier and who now was our daughter's staunchest defender, she asked the Roman Catholic Church to listen to her. The Vatican refused. Cardinal Ratzinger cited Statutes of Limitations. More than ten years had passed since the abuse took place. Her case was dismissed. Along with how many others?

Our daughter then asked the Swiss hierarchy to review her case. Our bishop addressed the issue, consulted with the other bishops in Switzerland, and finally offered an apology. At last our daughter felt listened to. She started down the long road of healing, after twenty-eight years of buried silence and then six long years of asking for justice. Thirty-four years. The scars are deep.

Abuse, pedophilia, secrecy—all of it within the church where Pierre and I and our family had felt at home. The impact shattered whatever complacency we'd had. And it shattered our image of the church. No longer was it our welcoming home. No longer did Pierre and I want to attend. Instead, come

Sunday we would ask ourselves how we could best spend the day. What would best nourish our faith and our relationship? Would we go to church or would we take a long walk together and draw strength from the nature around us? Where would we more easily find the image of our God? Still today we ask ourselves these questions. We answer as honestly as possible.

We want to remember the pieces of sea glass from the bottom of the sea that are tossed up on the shore and then start to glow. They show us how to confront the storms, how to ride the waves home to each other. How to live through the darkness and nestle deep in our love.

JOURNAL PRACTICE 12: STORMS AND DARKNESS

What storm in your relationship caused you to look inward?

- Was the storm sudden?

- Or did it build slowly?

- Did it hit both you and your partner with equal force?

- Were hurtful words spoken?

- Do you remember a few of them?

- What did you do to help each other cope?

- Was there healing?

- Was there new strength?

Dorothea Brande gives us guidance. She writes, "You are stirring latent memories, reaching down into the depths of your nature, releasing sensations and experience." Sometimes these episodes have been quite forgotten. Everything that has happened to you is of use. And if you do not let yourself be indifferent or uninterested in the process, you will find new material every day of your writing. And every day will take you deeper.

✺ SUGGESTION

Journaling opens the path to a better understanding of yourself, your partner, and your relationship. The path may meander—a few thoughts leading to a few more thoughts, as you stretch to translate the memory into words. And you continue the meander, as a river does. Or the path may pause with a full scene, with the details of the memory, the setting, the colors. Maybe what was said, a conversation. Let the path lead you to a deeper awareness of your own nature and the nature of your relationship.

And remember how the sea glass was tossed about by the waves and currents.

Close your eyes, breathe deeply, and write a journal entry about riding through a storm in your relationship. Take your time. Release the sensations gently.

Find your partner and share your words. Look inward together. Kindle the spark within to keep your relationship aglow.

NOURISHING THE SPARK

PIERRE AND I HAVE LEARNED THAT THE DEEPENING OF our relationship corresponds to our practice of quiet prayer or meditation. When we become more centered, more composed, our relationship becomes more centered, more composed. Now, in this Indian summer of our lives, we are able to devote a few moments of quiet each morning—Pierre in his office, me in my study—to reading, then sitting and being still. I turn to the words of Psalm 46, "Be still and know that I am God." We do this before breakfast, before we start our busy days. A prayer time without words. A resting in silence. Trusting that the small spark within us will continue to glow.

It was not so when the children were growing up and our lives were more hectic. An early-morning prayer practice was difficult. We looked for scattered moments of quiet during the day, and in the evening we paused with the children as we gave grace before dinner. We voiced our prayers for ourselves and those around us, as well as for what was going on in the world. Then we gave thanks for our love and family, for the sunshine, for whatever came into our minds. When the children left home, Pierre and I continued to give thanks before our evening meal. Meister Eckhart, the medieval theologian, preached that if we have only one prayer, it should be, "Thank you."

Along with our daily prayer, we respected the times of the liturgical calendar. There is a natural rhythm to slowing down on Sunday to offer praise and thanksgiving. To keep the

Sabbath. To remember to rest on the seventh day of the week. Our neighbors for many years were practicing Muslims from Kuwait. Living next door to them as they practiced Ramadan allowed us to grow not only in respect for their faith, but in a re-evaluation of our own faith. It made us think about the importance of fasting and discipline in our spiritual lives.

There were also the seasons of the liturgical year. Advent, awaiting Noel, waiting for the light in the longest nights of the year. It was in being a catechist that I deepened my own appreciation of Advent. At home, we made our own Advent calendars. We celebrated with joy the birth of Jesus, this child of God. Then came Lent, forty days to prepare for Easter, the promise of new life. When Easter arrived, we adopted a tradition from northern France and celebrated the holiday with the Easter bell, filled with little gifts for our children. During Lent, the bells do not ring, then on Easter Sunday they peel forth, bringing joy and carrying small surprises for the children. Celebrating these holidays together helped make prayer a part of our family life.

Another way we have found to nourish our inner lives is by drawing close to nature. Our poets and mystics teach us this. I think of Jelaluddin Rumi, "The breeze at dawn has secrets to tell you." Or Rainer Maria Rilke, "Often a star was waiting for you to notice it." I ask myself, when have we gone outside in the early morning to listen to the breeze? When have we gone for a walk at night to look at the stars? To find the brightest one? Nature calls us to rest ourselves in the beauty of the early morning, of the sky at night. When I am outside, be it in the morning, afternoon, or evening, and I take time to feel the proximity of the oak trees bordering the road, when I lift my eyes to follow their green branches up into the sky, I feel at one with them. I quiet down and trust the cycles of nature. I let it be my teacher.

I have shared this with Pierre, and now almost every day we take a short walk together. We stop in front of the oak trees spreading their branches, the maple trees slowly letting fall their autumn leaves. Or we stop on the hillside, with its vertical vineyards, overlooking the lake and the mountains beyond. There is a solitary bench at the far corner of the vineyard. After an initial moment of awe, we feel a sense of communion with nature, and also with one another. We are quiet, with a silent thank you for the beauty of everything that surround us.

Thich Nhat Hanh, the Vietnamese Buddhist monk, speaks of walking meditation. One step at a time. He writes, "Walking not to arrive, but just to walk.... Every step makes a flower bloom under our feet." Praying without words as we walk, making flowers bloom under our feet, along our way. We breathe in as we take a few steps, breathing in the earth, its scent, its density. Breathing in the creation, grateful for its gifts. Then we breathe out as we take a few more steps, giving back to the earth what we have taken, maybe asking forgiveness for not taking better care of it, for all the times we have plundered it. We have learned to walk this way. We follow a certain rhythm, breathing in as we take three or four steps, then breathing out three or four steps. The steady rhythm quiets us, empties our minds. We discover our oneness with the earth and our oneness with each other.

Pierre and I have also deepened our inner lives by reading books that stimulate our prayer life, our spirituality. Many years ago we together read *Hymn of the Universe* by Pierre Teilhard de Chardin. It challenged our traditional thinking and revitalized our faith. We saw the earth as the matrix of the Spirit. The spiritual power of matter. "Son of earth, steep yourself in the sea of matter, for it is the source of your life." We looked anew at the sea of matter, at the trees, the hills, the mountains around us. We looked anew at our own physical bodies. We were sons and daughters of the earth. All of creation was to be celebrated.

I remember another book that moved both of us deeply, *An Interrupted Life* by Etty Hillesum, the Dutch Jewish woman who kept a journal of her last two years in Amsterdam and then at the transit camp before facing death at Auschwitz at the age of twenty-nine. The book is an incredible testimony to her courage and strength as she continued to reclaim areas of peace in herself and to reflect it toward others until her death. "The more peace there is in us, the more peace there will be in our troubled world." Pierre and I continue to question our own individual faith and life in front of her authentic testimony. She calls us to attention.

Before ending this chapter about looking inward, I see still another way to nourish our inner lives, and that is to pay attention to our dreams. Often in the morning, at breakfast, Pierre and I ask each other if we dreamed, or rather if we remember a dream. I believe we dream most every night but we don't always remember our dreams. Yet they are stepping stones to a deeper life. I write down my dreams in my journal. How quickly they vanish when we don't write them down.

Pierre and I do not try to analyze our dreams, to tell each other this means this or that, but we give our dreams our attention, or rather our imagination. We ask each other how the dream felt, what are our emotions upon remembering it? Was there something in the dream that made one of us remember a recent or long-ago experience? Are there associations to what we are living or what we lived in the past? And are there amplifications, letting us follow the dream deeper into our imagination—what Jung would call the collective unconscious, that deep layer of myths, symbols, visions, and dreams accumulated over all time and place? Is there an image that opens the door to something more universal, to a fairytale, a painting? Something that stirs our imagination, awakens our creativity.

Our breakfast-table talk about dreams is a conversation, a sharing, a bit of alchemy as we look for the gold in the dream. I think of a dream like a plant. If I pull it up out of the earth and expose it to too much sunlight, it dries up. But instead, if I go into the dark to water its roots, it stays alive. It blossoms. So it is for a dream. If it is pulled up into too much light, into too much cerebral analysis, it dries up. Instead if I meet it in the dark, in the unconscious, and water it with my imagination, it will remain fresh and alive.

I recently had a dream where Pierre and I are walking to a lake. Our path leads us between high cliffs on either side. The passage becomes very narrow. We continue walking. Soon the passage opens, and the lake is before us. We are alone. The water is deep green and clear. We walk into it, fully dressed, and start swimming. We swim together further out into the middle of the lake. End of dream. I am always happy when I dream of water, and still more happy when I enter water. And this time I entered water with Pierre. I shared the dream with him. We stayed with the image of the two of us walking into the lake and swimming. For me it was an image of serenity and also of new creativity. I am heartened to go back to it, to be swimming in the clear green water. And to be swimming side by side with Pierre.

When Pierre and I share our dreams, they bring our hopes and fears into the open. Dreams, as C. G. Jung wrote, are "little hidden doors opening into the cosmic night of the unconscious." We get a glimpse into a deeper life below the surface in our relationship. Why do I feel good about this dream? I see it as us as a couple discovering our togetherness. Each of us becoming a fuller person. Each of us contributing to a fuller relationship.

Memories of listening, of walking, reading, sharing dreams, all ways to keep the spark within us alive. Seeing ourselves as pieces of sea glass, wanting to stay centered as the currents of life threaten to pull us under. Wanting to live with a contented spirit like Baucis and Philemon. And like the sea glass, wanting to shine from within.

JOURNAL PRACTICE 13:
NOURISHING THE SPARK

What ways have you found to nourish your inner life? It may be meditation, or walking, reading, sharing dreams, or hiking, camping, sailing. Choose one or say whatever comes to mind.

- When did you last do this?
- Where were you?
- Was your partner with you?
- What did you experience?
- What did you see or feel?
- Is it a practice?
- Something you do often?

A few more words from Dorothea Brande, "Creative writing is a function of the whole man." It involves both the conscious and the unconscious. The unconscious needs to flow freely, bringing at demand the treasures it has stored away. The conscious mind must combine and discriminate between these treasures without slowing the flow of the unconscious. Brande sees the unconscious as unwieldy but the writer can learn to tap into it. And she sees the conscious mind as meddlesome, but the writer can learn to train it. The writer learns to live with both.

🌸 SUGGESTION

Journal entries are steps along the path of self-discovery. As Brande explains, such writing is a two-fold exercise. To find the memory, you tap into your unconscious. Then to write the memory, you use your conscious mind. With practice, the writer learns to connect the unconscious to the conscious exercise of writing. To bring the two together.

Write a new journal entry, a memory from your unconscious, put into words by your conscious mind. Be relaxed. Remember writing is magic.

Try to find a way to make a habit of showing these pages to your partner. Of looking forward to this moment of sharing. Of doing so with a contented spirit.

Then put the pages together, "Memories of Looking Inward." Another chapter in your love story. Another chapter to hold in your hands.

Evergreen Ivy

CHAPTER FIVE

Growing: The Way
of Evergreen Ivy

Geneva, October 20

This week I had to put my journal writing aside in order to prepare the workshop on short stories that I gave yesterday. I was sorry to do this as I wanted to write an entry each day for a week. But to feel in touch with a room full of writers, to listen to the first lines of their stories, this made up for my frustration.

It is hard for me to balance my teaching and my writing. I love both. It's only in staying balanced myself that I can balance what I do. I know this and still I forget. I need my quiet prayer time, I need my daily walk. A balance between care of the soul, care of the body. When I do this, then the rest of my day, of my life, falls pretty much into place.

For now, on this Sunday afternoon, I am writing a journal entry about growing, another step to lasting love. How to keep growing even at our age. To remember that the river of life keeps flowing forward. That all is movement.

When Pierre and I went out this morning, I looked at the ivy on the wall by our front door. The leaves glistened in the sunlight. The vine is immense. It covers the whole wall. I focused on just a few leaves, seeing each single leaf shining, reaching upward, with little buds waiting to flower in winter. Each leaf a whole world in itself.

As I write, I see the ivy anew in my imagination. Each leaf a whole world. I, too, am a whole world in myself. And our marriage is a whole world, filled with memories which I am bringing back to life.

I think of Basho who wrote that poetry arises when we plunge deep enough into what we are looking at "to see something like a hidden light glimmering there." This is what I want to do with the images that I write about, with the nautilus shell, the maple leaf, the sunflower, the sea glass, and now the ivy. To plunge into them. And see a light glimmering.

In the pages ahead I listen to the ivy. I listen not just for myself but for the two of us. Two shoots of ivy, wanting to grow side by side. Wanting to send out new little buds and seeds.

This morning when we went out and when I looked at the ivy, we were going to church. So much has happened that has challenged our faith—not our faith in our God of love, but our faith in the Catholic Church. And more exactly in the structures of the Catholic Church. I am no longer comfortable within its walls. But the tradition has deep roots for Pierre. We try to go twice a month. I ask myself for how long.

Today it was our Sunday to go to church. A week ago we went for a long walk instead, up past the railroad tracks and into the woods where there is a small brook. Nature is becoming my church. The changing colors, the rushing water over the stones, the warm sun on my back, my liturgy.

And I return to the green ivy. It is my Sunday reading. I could make it my daily reading.

FINDING A BALANCE

IN THE FIRST CHAPTER ABOUT COURTSHIP, I REFER TO
the philosopher Heraclitus who wrote that you cannot step
into the same river twice; life is always moving on. Now in this
fifth chapter, I continue to write about moving on, about how a
relationship either progresses or declines. Goes forward or goes
backward. Even after more than half a century, it is still so for
Pierre and me. The river of life does not stand still.

The image I've chosen for this chapter is English ivy, a vine
that grows on the wall close to our front door. English ivy is
an evergreen. It flourishes and thrives all year round. Its sturdy
stems continue to climb upward, sending out aerial shoots that
hold on to the wall. So it is in our relationship. Over the years,
with its good moments and its less good moments, to make
our marriage work, we needed to continue to grow, to send out
aerial shoots to continue to climb.

In the early years of our marriage, Pierre and I wanted to
stay the way we were when we first fell in love. We wanted
that same romantic excitement, that same exhilarating rush
of emotion in our veins. Everything seemed to blossom. But
the early excitement lessened. We had to find new sources of
sparkle and romance. Like the ivy on the wall, we learned that
without growth, love withers. With growth, love blossoms.

This pattern of growth asked us to look for a sense of
balance, an equilibrium in our lives. There was a balance to
find between work and play. As I look back, when Pierre was

pursuing his career, keeping long hours, traveling every month, it was mostly all work. It was the same for me at home. I had my hands full with our children, moving from country to country, changing languages. There was little room for play. No lunch dates for just the two of us, no afternoon bike rides, no movies in the evening. We had to consciously look for time to play. We had to program moments of relaxation, find babysitters to let us get away. Both of us were set into our daily work habits. We forgot how it felt to relax for just a day, even for just an afternoon.

I remember when we moved to Geneva—Pierre absorbed in his new job, me absorbed in settling the seven of us into a small three bedroom apartment, we took the kids for a long weekend in the family chalet in the mountains. It wasn't planned. It just happened. And it was a great time for all of us. We played the game *la bête noire* outside in the evening, in the dark; we hunted for the "black beast," the one of us who was hiding alone. It's become our favorite family game. We play it outside or inside. And now we play it with our grandchildren. For years it's been a family tonic, making us relax, laugh, shout, run, and hide from each other.

Today, with the children gone, with the nine to seven office days gone, we need to find this balance between work and play. We could become addicted to our computer screens, each of us working, reading, and writing. I know I could write for hours. And Pierre also could sit at his computer, reading reports from the foundation where he works, scanning websites. This is a temptation for both of us. We need to get away from our desks

and our computers, we need to make time to enjoy ourselves—
to walk down to the lake, to cook a good meal together, to go
out for a movie or concert, or simply to sit down in our living
room with a good book.

There was also a balance to find between exercise and rest.
When we used to ski or play tennis together, this was easy
and fun and conducive to an active love life. Our bodies were
in shape. They called us to each other. Then with an injury to
my shoulder, we had to look for quieter sports to take pleasure
in together. There was swimming . We could do this regularly,
synchronizing our strokes. And there was walking. Pierre and
I have always enjoyed short brisk walks. The exercise is good
for us and frees our minds. But I still miss playing together
in doubles. Or trying to follow him as he slaloms beautifully
down a ski trail.

We are still learning to rest. To take time off, to go away for
a day, to be lazy on Sundays. To not feel we have to finish every
job we start at the designated time. To forget about deadlines,
to relax about having company and celebrating birthdays, to
leave the newspapers out and let the house be messy, to tell
ourselves it's all okay. To just be together and do nothing.

And so we practice. We look for ways to rest. For example
we are taking more time each evening to enjoy each other's
company. We are learning to cook together, appreciating each
other's presence and conversation as we chop carrots and
onions, then setting the table, lighting some candles and sitting

down to enjoy what we have prepared together. Afterwards we encourage each other to stay in the living room, and not to return to our computers and desks. To stay together, sometimes reading, sometimes listening to music. In winter oftentimes in front of a wood fire, watching the flames dance against the dark walls of the open fireplace.

We both need to remind ourselves that we can take time off. We are fortunate to live in lovely countryside. Even our small backyard is lovely. We could just sit for a while after a light lunch and look at the tall locust trees at the end of our yard, their spindly trunks reaching high over our heads and their white blossoms floating down upon us. We could listen to birdsong. We would like to learn to recognize the different birds that visit us. I have a book with photos of birds that come to this area. We could look at it as we linger after lunch in our backyard.

Now a memory of something we do. We walk down to the lake, out on the pier, here at Port Gitana, and we feed the ducks. Quickly the seagulls fly in, flocks of them, fluttering, jabbering, catching our pieces of bread before they fall to the ducks. When we have no bread left, all becomes quiet again. We are moved by the flurry of life and then the stillness. It's good to remember and to write about this. And to remind ourselves to do it again very soon.

And a very fresh memory, a murmuration—love this word—a flock of hundreds of starlings, rising and falling over the vineyards. Pierre and I were on our daily walk. We looked up and saw a cloud dancing, a cloud of birds, swooping down

135

over the field. At one moment they settled on the ground, all of them. Not one in the sky. Then up they went by common accord. We were stunned into silence.

I think of still another balance—between privacy and community. When we spent too much time alone with just each other, it stifled the way we listened to each other. I began to think that I knew exactly what Pierre would say, how he would react. And it was the same for Pierre. We started to ask each other fewer questions. We needed the company of our children, of others. I needed to see Pierre not only in tête-à-tête, but also in the middle of others. To listen to what he says, to feel anew his energy.

Likewise, if we found ourselves constantly with family and friends, we experienced a similar dulling of the relationship. We ended up paying attention to everyone around us and less to each other. I could be at a dinner with friends, engaged in conversation, and overlook the presence of Pierre. As a result, a certain superficiality entered our relationship. On the surface all was well, we thought we were doing fine, but underneath there was no new growth. We needed to find both moments alone and moments with others.

Respecting the rhythm of growth. Looking to balance work and play, exercise and relaxation, time alone and time with others. Looking to slow down and enjoy each other's company. To follow the example of the two independent stalks of ivy growing upward side by side.

JOURNAL PRACTICE 14:
FINDING A BALANCE

Go back in your memory to times of work, then times of play.
Choose a time of play.

- What was the setting?

- Were you outside?

- In a place you go to often?

- Were you and your partner alone?

- Was it invigorating?

- Or relaxing?

- Or both?

- Did you feel close to the other?

Annie Dillard, in The Writing Life, *opens with, "When you*
write, you lay out a line of words..." A line of words that leads
you into a new place where you will lay out another line of words.
She compares the line of words to a miner's pick. You chip away
and dig a path to follow. You find yourself in new territory. "You
make the path boldly and follow it fearfully." You write each line
boldly. The memories are yours. And you write fearfully because
you don't know where each line will lead you.

🍀 SUGGESTION

In journal writing, you go into the unknown. Don't figure
out in advance what you will write, where you will go. Let the

writing take you there. One line of words at a time. Be patient. Be curious. Let each line take you deeper. You discover a new place, new colors, new emotions, you write about them and you move on. Another line. You follow your words. Another new place. Your writing becomes braver.

Start to lay out one line of words. Then another line of words. Until you have a short journal entry, a memory of play.

Another page of writing to read to your partner. Maybe plan a couple's date and share memories of play and work. Memories of finding a balance in order to continue growing together.

THE ARTS OF COMPROMISE
AND COMMUNICATION

Pierre and i did not always want to do the same thing at the same time. We needed to find compromises. Looking back to times when our relationship seemed stuck, we learned there were different dimensions of compromise: physical, spiritual, and social. When we paid attention to these aspects, we gave a new liveliness to our relationship. We had smoother sailing in spite of rough weather.

For example, when Pierre and I are confronted—I switch to the present tense because it is still our reality—with a crisis, when we are arguing obstinately, each of us certain in our rightness, perhaps about how to react to an adult child's request, it may be the physical dimension that comes to the rescue of our relationship. We can put the difficulty aside until bedtime. As we lie close together, our tempers soften and that's when we find a solution.

On another occasion, it may be the spiritual aspect that quiets the crisis. We can look for quiet moments of dialogue, a mutual soul-searching. Pierre and I will take a walk together and slowly find the words that heal. We will be able to explain our response together.

Another time, it may be the social dimension. We will turn to our family and friends for new ideas and fresh energy. They will help us to get some needed distance and put the situation in perspective. We can create new steps in our relationship.

Buoyancy, lightness, enthusiasm versus rigidity, heaviness, despondency.

And so we continue to learn the art of compromise. If the ivy cannot send out its shoots to the right, it sends them to the left. And it will keep growing. So it is in a relationship. When there is a confrontation of two different wills, when Pierre and I are at loggerheads, we have to discover a new way to grow. We look for a middle ground. Even though we started long ago looking for the middle ground, somewhere in the middle of the ocean between France and America, that place still needs to be found.

Pierre is more of an extrovert than I, and this guides his choices of pastimes. He would choose to go out more often to the movies, theater, and concerts. I would choose to stay home more often. And his choice of what movies, what plays to see, would also be different from mine. So would his choice of vacation spots. There is a give and take here for both of us. When we both participate in the give and take, there is mutual enrichment.

Some compromises have evolved over the years. A simple example concerns our eating habits. The French prefer their big meal at noon, and they are in general content with soup and cheese in the evening. This was not my preference and it continues to not be my preference. During our child-rearing years, with different lunch hours for our kids, I stuck to a light lunch at noon: sandwiches and a salad. Our family dinner was in the evening. Pierre had his hot meal at work and another at home. We managed. Now that there are just the two of us, we have his soup and cheese at lunch, and my bigger hot meal in the evening.

❧

In tandem with the art of compromise is the art of communication. It's in discussing our differences that we find our compromises. In each of the earlier chapters, I have written about talking and listening to one another. It is this daily dialogue that keeps a relationship evergreen like the ivy.

We fell in love talking and listening to each other. And to help us stay in love, early on we established our habit of monthly dates. This monthly habit has been a walking stick for both of us on the path to lasting love. And it has been a lifesaver during the difficult times.

Early in our marriage, we also put in place yearly brief honeymoons. Honeymoons for courtship. But also for deep sharing and listening. Sometimes there are things that we do not want to share except in very special circumstances. Communication needs to be cultivated—watered and nourished. And sometimes this nourishing may happen during a weekend of lovemaking. When I wanted something more in our relationship, when I was dissatisfied, sometimes it was only when I was in Pierre's arms that I found the words to express myself.

There are also everyday moments of communication. To stop from time to time in our daily routine to be sure the other is with us, that we are understanding each other. To ask the other if he or she is okay. To ask ourselves if we are okay?

Are we listening to each other? There are two of us. I am not alone living my day. There need to be bridges of communication built into our daily lives. Moments to stop and say to the other, What are you thinking about? What would you like to do this evening? What are you looking forward to? And to open up in return. To keep learning about each other. And in so doing, to keep learning about ourselves.

To love is to grow. To let the ebb and flow of our lives nourish our relationship. Like the ivy, we continue to look for ways to keep growing forward together.

JOURNAL PRACTICE 15:
COMPROMISE AND COMMUNICATION

Find a memory of when you looked for a compromise.

- Was it long ago?

- Was there a confrontation?

- Or was there a quiet sharing?

- What was the weather?

- Stormy or sunny?

- Do you remember listening to the other?

- Do you remember a few words you said?

- Did you learn something?

Annie Dillard writes about the line of words, "The line of words is a fiber optic, flexible as wire; it illumines the path." She suggests that your lines of writing are light pipes to transmit images. They will illumine your path. You probe with the line of words, peer into the dark, look for signposts, get lost, and find your way anew. This is the writer's life.

❧ SUGGESTION

A few words of dialogue can reveal more about the writer than lines and lines of description and exposition. "Honey, I'm sorry…" says a great deal about the speaker. When you include a conversation in your journal entry, you can put it simply in the middle of your paragraph. No quotation marks are needed. You, the writer, are remembering an exchange of words. Or you can be more formal and set up the conversation as a dialogue, with indentations and quotation marks. A new indent for each new response. Either way is possible. Either way you may discover something new about yourself.

Close your eyes, see the memory, and start writing. Do not worry about where you are going. Your words will show you the path. Maybe include a bit of dialogue, a few words you exchanged with your partner.

Ask you partner to listen to your page. And create in this way a new memory of talking and listening together.

THE SEASONS OF LOVE

To continue growing in love, pierre and i have found a teacher in the natural world. The closer we grow to nature, the more readily our relationship grows. We have learned that love has its seasons—spring, summer, fall, winter. Just as day and night and light and darkness are patterns of growth, so are the seasons. Pierre and I remind each other that after the rainstorms of spring, there will be the blossoms and fruits of summer. That when the autumn leaves fall, they return to their roots. That winter promises us rest; we will be snug inside together when there is cold and snow outside.

When spring comes, Pierre and I look for new life. The forsythia blossoms, a splash of bright yellow in our backyard. The lilac flowers. We get out lighter clothing, muted shades. We shed our heavy dark sweaters and don soft wraps of light blue, light green. Time to plant tulips and daffodils in our gardens and nurse them into bloom. We plan short holidays, a trip somewhere. We are restless and want to discover something new. This is springtime—usually April and May. But whenever there is restlessness, there is "spring fever," no matter what month.

Then summer, when the ivy leaves spread out wide and confident. In a relationship also summer brings a sense of satisfaction. Pierre and I live more fully in the present. We welcome the sun-filled days, we feel all right with each other. It's time to put out the garden table and chairs, to eat outdoors and relax in the sun. Time to cut the grass and appreciate the hydrangeas that will continue to flower into the fall. We enjoy long days of staying put. Our pace slows down, is more relaxed. We greet the early morning, catching moments of happiness, like children catching beach balls at the seaside. And come the late afternoon, we stay outside in the last rays of sunshine, appreciating the early evening breeze, watching the light change to blue before it darkens.

The wind rustles the leaves; autumn is coming. We watch the leaves turn bright yellow and red. Coming from New York and remembering the late Indian summers as the maple trees set the yards and streets ablaze in color makes this a favorite time for me. It's time to take stock, time for an annual couple's date. We ask ourselves where we are, where we have been, where we are going. It's time to wonder why the ivy stays deep green. To realize that we, too, can stay deep green. Autumn moments in our relationship are moments for revision. Summer and all the bright sun-filled days are finished. We know that winter is ahead of us. We breathe in deeply, grateful to be the two of us together as we soon confront the cold and the long dark nights of winter.

The long dark nights come. Amazingly the ivy shoots grow little buds and flowers and seeds in winter. We can do the same. As we knuckle down, we think of all that they want to do in the spring. The shoots send out little messages, plant little seeds. We sit in front of a warm wood fire, look at the glowing red flames, and share our thoughts and dreams. "Everything is gestation," writes Rainer Maria Rilke, "and then bringing forth." We will bring forth. Spring is around the corner. But for now, we put on our heavy woolen sweaters and add an extra blanket to our bed. We once again grow accustomed to the long hours of darkness. Dark when we get up in the morning, dark when we return home in late afternoon. The darkness teaches trust. Trust in knowing that the light will follow, that spring will come.

As I write this, we are moving into winter. We have lived those crisp cool autumn days. The maple leaves have fallen to the ground. We walk on them, we feel them beneath our shoes, we hear them crunch, we smell their fresh scent of earth mixed with rain and wind. I remember all the leaves in the yards of my childhood. I remember raking them into piles. I want to do this again, to make piles of leaves, to play in them, to toss them back up into the air. I tell Pierre to walk into the piles, to kick and toss the leaves upward. To toss ourselves upward. And then to settle back on the ground and return to our roots, knowing that new life will again appear. That spring will come.

There are many seasons of love throughout a lifetime—over fifty-five years of our long marriage. Springtime, the excitement and sheer joy of the first years, the heightened romance, the shared dreams, the world around us seeming to blossom. We moved through summer, resting on our laurels. Then slowly our rainbow-colored glasses clouded over. Autumn, not everything was perfect. We saw in the fading sunlight the other's weaknesses. We started to quarrel with each other over nothing. And moving into winter, instead of holding each other close, we turned away from each other. We wondered how we ever thought we could get along.

According to sociologists, this is the *U* curve in long relationships. We were in our mid forties when we were at the bottom of the curve. I still had the six kids pulling me in all directions. And Pierre had his profession weighing on him as heavily as his wife and six children. The walks we took as a way of communicating, had become a way of arguing. But we kept walking, and we kept trying to find common ground, a compromise, courtship, commitment. Our monthly dates became weekly. Slowly we started to climb up the other side of the *U* curve. We started to listen anew to each other. We started to look at what we appreciated in each other.

And now today we are living an Indian summer. We linger with the autumn leaves, bright reds and yellows. We know winter is ahead of us. We hold on to all that is good and wonderful in our relationship. We know that the ivy on the wall close to our front door stays green all year round.

JOURNAL PRACTICE 16:
SEASONS OF LOVE

*Remember something you did together in your favorite season.
Something outside in nature.*

- Where were you?
- What were the colors?
- The sounds?
- Could the experience have happened in a different setting?
- Could it have happened in a different season?
- What were your emotions?
- What role did nature play?

*Dillard reassures the writer. "Words lead to other words and
down the garden path." Start with a word, then add another
word. Like a painter, you adjust the paints and hues. The
materials are stubborn. There are no secrets to show the way.
Only the page. "The page which you cover slowly... that page will
teach you to write." Dillard writes that there is another way of
saying this. When you chop wood, aim for the chopping block.
Not for the wood.*

❧ SUGGESTION
Consider green ivy. Look at one green leaf. How confident it
is, how bright and daring it is. Let it teach you to be bright and
daring in your writing. Close to the stem, the leaf will grow a

bud that will flower and the flower will contain a seed. As you journal, be confident in what you are doing. Start with a word, then another word. A line, then another line. Do not worry about where you are going. Read aloud your words. Read aloud one line. Does it lead you to another line? Be bright and daring like the ivy leaf.

Write for ten minutes. Imagine the words taking you down the garden path. Imagine yourself the painter. Mix the colors.

Show the scene, and the words, to your spouse or partner. Invite him or her to accompany you down the garden path.

STANDING FREE SIDE BY SIDE

I HAVE READ THAT IN LATE FALL, WHEN THE IVY IS ADULT, its shoots are sturdier and stronger, without small aerial roots. They no longer attach themselves to the wall, to the rock or the tree. Instead they are self-supporting and stand free. They raise upward to the light. I have seen this happen. And I have seen how in early winter they flower, small clusters of yellowish-white flowers, with dark berries that ripen in late winter. Come spring, the seeds are dispersed by the birds that draw close to eat the berries. It is an entire life cycle, played out on the wall for me to watch, showing me how nature runs its course.

I want to focus here on when the shoots become self-supporting, when they stand free and independent. We could be married for more than one hundred years and still not be free to grow side by side. When did I find myself strong enough to no longer hold on to the wall, to no longer cling to all the hand grips? To be self-supporting? It was only after many years of holding on to the handrails we had put in place early in our marriage. When Pierre and I decided we wanted a large family, we accepted the traditional roles of husband and wife. I would stay home and raise a family. He would go out into the world and earn what was necessary to support us. I depended upon his work and profession, I was not self-supporting. I realize that in accepting this early division of labor, we eliminated a large source of conflict between competing professions. It would take years of child-bearing and child-raising, before I realized I did not have to hold so tightly to the stucco wall.

I could let go and grow strong alongside my husband. I could decide to save time for myself each day. It's what I did as I was turning fifty. I stopped rushing around for the last two children who were still at home. They were old enough to rush around for themselves. I stopped volunteering at their schools and in their activities. I stopped thinking I had to take care of all my neighbors. Instead I could give myself the couple of hours gained each day. I could read, I could write. For my fiftieth birthday I went to my first writers' workshop. It was two weeks away from my family, away from daily chores. I entered a new exciting creative world. I was no longer holding on tight to the railings in our relationship. I was growing straight up alone.

This encouraged Pierre to also let go of his set pattern. He could take time for himself. Some of the things he had put aside—sailing, mountain climbing, piano lessons—he could now do. Life opened up. Pierre went mountain climbing in the French Alps with his oldest son. I stayed home and wrote. Another time he went rafting down the Colorado River with an old school chum from Grenoble. Again I stayed home and wrote. And it was okay. Now each June when we travel together to the States, I go to teach at a writers' conference, Pierre goes to sail with friends on the Connecticut coast.

In today's world, the roles are evolving. We see our children and their friends assuming autonomy so much earlier. We see our daughters continuing to be self-supporting whether they are married and have children or not. We see our sons taking more time from their work to be with their children. Some professions lend themselves more easily to this. Our piano-playing son is able to have more time at home than many fathers. We see fathers and mothers raising their children together. Recently we were visiting friends in Sweden. Their son came to show us their new baby, a second child. He brought both children for the visit because his wife was working. In Sweden, sixteen months of paid childcare leave are given to the parents, and at least two of them have to be taken by the father. The son was relaxed, happy to present his children to us, promising next time it would be his wife's turn. Two stalks of ivy, each self-supporting.

※

Sometimes two strong ivy shoots may confront subzero weather, a draught, fierce winds, or simply angry crows fighting in their leaves. Then these two adult shoots of ivy reach for one another and put out little roots to hold on tight once again. When the angry crows were Pierre and me, when one of us wasn't happy and wanted to do something his or her own way, we realized the need for new roots; we needed to come together in order to look for ways to be supportive together.

"For better or for worse," Pierre and I promised each other. There are times when it seemed for worse. Why, we asked ourselves. Why do I have to continue to do this? Why do I have to give up my pleasure? Sometimes when I find myself isolated here in Switzerland, or in France where we spend many of our holidays at the family chalet in the Alps, I ask myself why I left America. Why am I living in a foreign country? Even after fifty years of living abroad, this still happens. My roots remain deeply American. And when I start asking myself these questions, I have to be very careful that these questions do not become, Why did I marry a Frenchman? Why did I ever think I could live my life in his country?

And it is the same for Pierre. Why this constant conflict? This different way of doing things? Why do I live with this person who is so foreign to the way I was brought up? And so many other questions, almost all coming down to one: Why did I marry an American?

When this becomes our inner dialogue, it is time for a couple's date. I need to share my disquiet, my buried feelings of not belonging. I need to explain to my dear husband that it is not him but rather the country, the foreign country. And he needs to share his frustration at having someone at his side who is so different, someone he never imagined he would choose to be his wife. And together we will look for ways to help us appreciate all that is good in each other and all that is good where we live—the children, the friends, the lake, the mountains. There is so much, so very much. We need a couple's date, and sometimes a weekend date.

We need a weekend to grow together. With time for courtship. To court and be courted. To seduce and be seduced. I need to see everything that I love about him. To try to be everything that he loves about me. To go for short walks wherever we find ourselves. To linger over our meals listening to the others' words. To feel his hand on my back. To respond.

GROWING: THE WAY OF EVERGREEN IVY

And to look outward anew. To discover and experience something different.

I remember when we did this about fifteen years ago, we were in our sixties. We were vacationing on the Greek island of Paros. We rented a scooter and rode around the entire island. By late afternoon, when it would have been prudent to return quickly to our small inn, we were still zipping along the seaside when a sudden storm burst. I wrapped my arms around Pierre and held on tight as he took us back in the pelting rain. We shivered in fright, but also in excitement at our ability to outsmart the storm gods at our age.

That small fragile flower that grows on the ivy plant in winter will give forth its seeds in spring. And there will be still more green leaves, more shoots, more flowers. From our spring and summer storms, Pierre and I have emerged more serene and more trusting. I sit at my desk upstairs in my study, and I write. Downstairs, Pierre plays the piano. Two adult shoots growing side-by-side, grateful for our love.

JOURNAL PRACTICE 17:
STANDING SIDE BY SIDE

Find a memory of standing free and independent, yet side by side.

- What was the activity that gave you independence?

- How old were you?

- Did the activity open a new world?

- What did you feel on your own?

- Have you continued?

- Was your partner interested?

- Was it easy to share the experience?

- Did he or she also find something new?

- Is it easy to stand side by side?

Annie Dillard describes the writing life as "life at its most free."
Not freedom in the sense of wild acting out, but freedom in the
sense of finding yourself. Feeling free to be yourself. Free to write
about what you find interesting. "You were made and set here
to give voice to this, your own astonishment." Discover through
writing what it is that interests you the most. Probe the mystery
of your life. Write to uncover its meaning.

✿ SUGGESTION

Journal entries can be anything. You may shape them as you
wish. If you write them as stories, as narratives of personal
history, start with the beginning, the desire on the part of the

narrator. What did you want? What desire or need prompted the personal experience? Then the middle part of the story, the experience of fulfilling your desire. What were the difficulties that you encountered? The story keeps building. And the third part of the story, the resolution, what James Joyce called the epiphany. What did you discover? This is called the narrative arc. It exists also in journal writing.

Write your journal entry perhaps in the form of a narrative. A sentence for the beginning, a few more sentences in the middle, and then a short outcome.

Find the right time to sit down with your partner and enjoy sharing your story together.

Put the four pages—Finding a Balance, Compromise and Communication, Seasons of Love, Standing Side by Side— together with the title "Growing." They tell the story of your love.

A Clear Pond

CHAPTER SIX

Wellbeing: The Pond of Memory

Geneva, October 21

It is good to be back writing a journal entry in the morning. My image for the chapter is a green pond, remembered from my childhood in Briarcliff Manor. The pond was in the center of my village. Wonderfully green and peaceful, it welcomed me all year round.

Ponds speak to me of how I would like to see our home. A place of wellbeing. Not only peaceful but also healthy. So I wish it to be for our relationship, peaceful and healthy.

This past summer when Pierre and I were walking at the end of a valley in the French Alps, we came upon a small clear pond surrounded by fir trees and spruce. Stunted shrubs and wild Alpine flora covered the edges. We sat on a granite boulder off to the side of the pond and rested. The water was different shades of green, reflecting the bushes and trees high around it.

As we sat on the rock, looking at the mountain pond in the middle of the firs and spruces, I experienced something very

Zen-like. A moment of clear seeing; nothing else intruded upon my vision.

I did not think about it as being an experience of Zen. It is only now in writing about the memory that I am uncovering its meaning. D. T. Suzuki, a Zen master, writes that in such an experience, a "hitherto closed screen" is lifted and a new vista opens up. That is what happened. A screen lifted, and I saw wellbeing.

In writing this, I think about the different ponds I have seen, starting with one that I remember from my childhood village. I ask myself, what distinguishes a pond from a lake? On the Internet, I learn that it is not necessarily the size, but rather the composition of the water, one permitting plant life, the other not. Ponds are typically shallow in order to let light pass down deep enough for plants to grow on the surface and below.

And so the deep green. The color that Christian mystic Hildegard of Bingen called "viriditas." The greening power of nature. That creative capacity and beauty that she saw in her beloved Rhineland where she established her monastery. Where she transcribed her visions, composed her music, healed with herbs, and preached viriditas. Freshness, fruitfulness, seeing it as an attribute of the Creator.

I have always liked the word. It's a Latin word first used by Gregory the Great to describe spiritual health. And then by Augustine, to describe mental health. I like how Hildegard used it, the lush greening power of nature. The lushness of all the creation. The lushness of our Creator.

And I am back to wellbeing. To my pond, to my chapter, to Pierre and me. We want to be well. We want our relationship to be well.

MY CHILDHOOD POND AND ZEN

THERE IS A ZEN-LIKE QUALITY THAT ENTERS INTO lasting love. A sense of wellbeing. This Zen-like quality lets us live our love with confidence, assuring us a constancy in our relationship. It is Basho Matsuo, the Japanese poet and Zen disciple, who wrote, "Sitting quietly, doing nothing, Spring comes, and the grass grows by itself." When there is wellbeing in a relationship, the grass grows by itself. Love blossoms on its own.

I remember a clear, green pond from my childhood, its banks overgrown with vegetation. Its still surface mirrored the bushes and willow trees surrounding it. The memory of the pond centers me, as it centered me in my childhood. It was a sheltered place, a refuge, in the middle of my small village. The pond was close to my school and not far from my house. A ten-minute walk. I rested alongside of it, looking deep into the transparent water. My little world was in its place. As I grew up, traveled to France, moved around Europe, raised children, I missed my childhood pond.

I was no longer sure everything was in its place. Sometimes I wondered where I was, what I was doing. When the kids crowded around me each morning, I turned to Pierre—a morning kiss, an implicit pledge of love, a pause to hold on to the rest of the day. He was my green pond. I needed those moments of togetherness, of centering. I needed to feel our love as a place of safekeeping. Even now, late in life and without the children crowding around me at home, I still need to feel that our relationship is a protected refuge, the green pond of my childhood.

Seeing our relationship as a refuge is a lesson in Zen, a lesson in awareness, in holding on to the essential and letting go of the rest. Thich Nhat Hanh, the Vietnamese Zen master, author of many excellent wise books, teaches us to cultivate the mind of love. To learn to cherish each present moment in a relationship. To look with the mind of love at each other. "People deal too much with the negative, with what is wrong." He suggests that we try to see positive things. "To just touch those things and make them bloom."

And so it is that in remembering the good times of our marriage, Pierre and I want to make them bloom. In cultivating those moments that nourish our sense of wellbeing, we learn what Zen masters call clear seeing. We focus on what makes our love alive. We pay deep attention to each other. We wake in the morning with a kiss, opening our arms to each other and to a new day. And we look for ways to welcome each other at the end of the day, to listen to each other, to share what we have done, what we have discovered. Maybe I'll have arranged a few flowers on the dining table, and one of us will light the candles. Mindful gestures transform our evening meals into small agapes, love feasts that continue to keep our relationship fresh and vibrant.

Zen masters say that seeing clearly is like holding up a mirror. The mirror reflects only what is in front of it, not what it "thinks" it sees. Similarly, with clear seeing I see our relationship as it is, without all the trappings around it. I see it as the two of us in love, without the interference of one thousand other things.

Zen also teaches us contentment. If we clearly see the positive things, we are more easily content. We worry less about the negative things, about what we did or didn't do yesterday, about what we will do or won't do tomorrow. We learn to live more fully the present moment. Our contentment overflows. It ripples outward to our families and friends. Just as when we throw a stone in the pond and the ripples circle outward, so, too, our composure becomes contagious.

We want to share our feelings of good will with our children and our grandchildren, with our neighbors and our friends. We go to them, they come to us. And together we are able to create moments of good-heartedness that are life-giving.

When we live in this Zen way, our home becomes like my childhood pond, a welcoming haven. Not only are we living in the present moment, appreciating each day, but, from our Western tradition, we can remember Meister Eckhart's teaching to say the one prayer that he deemed essential: thank you.

JOURNAL PRACTICE 18:
CONTENTMENT

Find a memory of when you and your partner were truly content and peaceful.

- Where were you?
- What time of year was it?
- And what time of day?
- What was the weather?
- Were you and your partner alone?
- What did you say?
- Did you draw close to one another?

I turn to Thomas Merton, Trappist monk and author, who kept a journal throughout his years at Gethsemani, his Trappist monastery. In a journal entry from September 1, 1949, he wrote, "To put myself down on paper, with the most complete simplicity and integrity—masking nothing." He knows that this will be very hard because he is all mixed up in illusions and attachments. These, too, he will have to put down on paper, but without exaggeration or breast-beating. He will put them down honestly.

✦ SUGGESTION

In expressing your memories as journal entries, you are writing as simply and honestly as you can. You are exploring an experience to find its meaning. This genre of writing is called creative nonfiction or literary nonfiction. It is the same form as personal essays or memoir. You are writing about something you lived, hence "nonfiction," and you are bringing it alive, describing the scene with vivid details, maybe including dialogue—hence the word "creative" or "literary." It is essential to do so honestly.

Describe this experience of contentment. See it anew. Live it anew. Maybe include a bit of dialogue. Try to convey the warmth of the shared wellbeing and peace.

This is a good page to share and enjoy with your spouse or partner. Relive it together. Plan to do so again.

SPRINGS OF RESPECT, TRUST, AND FORGIVENESS

My childhood pond was a welcoming habitat for plants and fish alike. The water remained a verdant green all summer long. *Viriditas.* Greenness. The greening power of nature described by Hildegard of Bingen. She saw the greenness of the Rhineland as life-giving. It was the color of creation, "earth's lush greening." I believe there is something like *viriditas* in a lasting relationship. A greenness that is life-giving to its partners and to its entourage.

There were no visible streams flowing into my childhood pond, only overgrown banks and bushes with willow trees bending low over the water. I appreciated its greenness without wondering how this happened. Later I learned that instead of surface inlets and outlets, instead of a stream flowing in and out, some ponds are fed by underground springs. Fresh water circulates from hidden springs. Such ponds develop self-contained ecosystems. So it was for the pond in my childhood village. I think it is the same for a lasting relationship. I would like to think that our marriage is such a self-contained ecosystem, fed by hidden springs.

One of the hidden springs would be respect, the respect each of us has for the other. It is respect that contributed to drawing Pierre and me together the year we met at Grenoble. We looked up to each other and wanted to get to know the other's thoughts and opinions. Then in the early years of our marriage, this respect grew as we continued to appreciate what each other were doing. I watched what Pierre was doing at the European Commission. And he watched as I handled our growing children.

So it is today as I follow Pierre's work at the Swiss foundation, where he contributes his skills and experience in evaluating different projects in favor of handicapped children around the world. Likewise he is supportive and respectful of my writing and remains my loyal reader. We have worked together on this book about our marriage, both of us wanting to share what we learned in our fifty-five years together. This has generated a spring of fresh water in our relationship, letting us relive many of the good moments. There is a healthy pride that each of us feels for the person we love.

Pierre and I know that when our relationship grows stagnant, we have to pay more attention to our individual selves and growth. We need to open the spring of respect. To keep our minds sharp. To find things that each of us does well. When one of us comes home content, excited about something we did, we bring home new energy. Likewise, to keep our spirit alive, we encourage each other to find quiet moments during the day, to make time for the practice of prayer and meditation. And we continue to share our reading and reflections about living and deepening our faith.

These are ways we have found to replenish our respect for each other. And this takes me back to my childhood pond. I see it fresh and clear, a welcoming habitat for both plants and fish. So may it be for our relationship.

☙

Side by side with the underground spring of respect is the spring of trust. Here I return to our marriage vows. Vows that Pierre and I renew implicitly each day, as we choose to love one another. Vows that we renew also with our monthly dates, taking the time to listen to each other, to see where we are in our relationship. Vows that we can more formally renew on special occasions. This is something we did on our fortieth wedding anniversary, when we returned to the church in Pocantico Hills in New York where we were married. We stood together at the altar, alone in the church, and renewed our vows to love and support each other. We gave thanks for each child and grandchild. It is this trust that has let Pierre and me live with a feeling of serenity and wellbeing, that has given us confidence in our relationship.

But when one of us betrays that trust, the underground source is blocked. The fresh water stops flowing into the relationship. I need to feel that Pierre remains loyal to me, and Pierre needs to feel that I remain loyal to him. I am not thinking only about the sexual level. I am thinking about loyalty on all levels. Loyalty in discussions with our children. Not to partake in criticism when the other is not there. And in discussions with friends and acquaintances, not to indulge in gossip about the other, not even to listen to it. It is this loyalty that keeps the spring of trust open.

When there is betrayal, whether it involves family or finances or infidelity, the sense of wellbeing is shattered. The wounded partner no longer knows how to relate to the other person. Pierre and I have been very fortunate not to have experienced this loss of trust. However we have seen it close at hand when, within our family, we saw a relationship break. It is like when someone breaks their leg and then tries to walk. The break first has to be repaired. For months we watched a couple suffer, unable to come back together. Then slowly they started to create new moments of togetherness which led them to remember earlier moments of togetherness. First the spring of respect began to refill. Then, more slowly, the spring of trust. We watched as husband and wife started to heal their wounds and come back together.

When husband and wife enjoy the wellbeing that comes from respect and trust, there is a constancy that can be counted upon. And I return to my pond that remains nourishing and life-giving in the middle of the bushes and the willow trees. So is it for Pierre and me. There may be tension and disquiet, but we stay confident in our trusting love.

Along with the springs of respect and trust, I see a third hidden spring that has to flow. The spring of forgiveness. Pierre and I continue to get angry with each other—sometimes very angry. When I am on his back all day, chiding him, at some point he loses his temper. And when he keeps on not listening, I lose mine. We stop speaking to each other. Pierre picks up the newspaper, and I bristle and brood. Fortunately our years of monthly dates come to our rescue. We look for an opening to explain and to say we are sorry. We wait for a sign that the other is ready to hear our apology. Then we go out for a monthly date. But only when we are ready to practice forgiveness.

Forgiveness takes patience. Patience with oneself and with the other. I am learning to not force a discussion when there has been a disagreement. My impulse has been to talk it over right away. To find an understanding, a solution. But Pierre prefers to wait until his emotions are calmer, until there's quiet. It has taken me years to appreciate his need to wait and to see that nothing is lost in waiting. Instead something is gained. A strong spring of clear water infuses our pond of love.

When our love is trusting and forgiving, there is kindheartedness in the home. We more readily enjoy each other's company. The home becomes a haven, like my green childhood pond, fed by the springs of respect and trust and forgiveness.

JOURNAL PRACTICE 19:
RESPECT, TRUST, FORGIVENESS

Go back in your memory to an experience when you felt respect or trust or forgiveness for your partner. Choose one, perhaps forgiveness.

- Was it long ago?
- What brought it about?
- Did you talk it over?
- Maybe on a couples date?
- Was it difficult to say, "I'm sorry"
- Did your partner reciprocate?
- What was the outcome?

In another early journal entry, Thomas Merton wrote about a moment of clarity. "I shall remember the time and place... clouds hung low on the horizon, the outcrops of hard yellow rock in the road, the open gate..." He remembers standing on rock. He remembers being gathered up in clarity. He was writing about a moment of grace, of freedom. The open gate. Nothing else mattered.

❧ SUGGESTION
Journal writing can be seen as a Zen practice, clear seeing. Try to quiet yourself before starting to write. Close your eyes and empty your mind of distractions. If a thought or worry

comes, let it go. Then see anew on the screen of your mind the experience that you are going to write about. If you see it clearly, you will write it clearly. Clear seeing and clear writing go hand in hand. Another Zen suggestion is to have beginner's mind. To write with a beginner's mind, as if you are living the experience for the first time. Journal writing then becomes meditative.

Write the place and date of this new journal entry. Describe your experience of feeling forgiveness. The moment of clarity.

Find a good time, maybe during a couples date, to share your memory with your partner. Read your page and see if your partner remembers the same moment. Speak to each other about forgiveness.

SANCTUARY, SOLITUDE, SILENCE

PIERRE AND I LIVE SIDE BY SIDE IN FULL CONFIDENCE. WE feel safe in the presence of the other. We can let down our defenses and be ourselves. We do not need to impress each other. This is such a wonderful gift of a trusting relationship. We are loved for who we are. Our home is a place of safety.

We remember the goddess of the hearth, Hestia, the first born of the Olympian gods and goddesses in ancient Greece. Zeus gave her the keys to Mount Olympus where she faithfully remained, tending the sacred fire. When the other gods and goddesses went down to earth, she stayed at home, waiting to welcome them back. Every house had a hearth dedicated to the Goddess. The days began and ended with a prayer requesting that Hestia protect and care for the family. Similarly the meals began and ended with an offering to her. Hestia's flame made the house into a true home, a place where both family and guests found sustenance, comfort, and warmth.

Likewise every city had a public hearth sacred to Hestia where the fire was never allowed to go out because it represented the energy of life. If a new city were to be founded, coals and embers were carried from the hearth of the mother city to kindle the fire in the hearth of the new city. In Rome, the goddess was known as Vesta. Her flame was tended by the Vestal Virgins. Her fire made sacred the place where it dwelled.

It is this flame of love that lets Pierre and me feel a warm security in our relationship, that lets us both feel free.

We can willingly let the other pursue his or her pleasure, and we can willingly do the same. I do not need to worry about what Pierre is doing. Sometimes during an outing or an evening with friends, each of us can be fully engaged in conversation with someone else. We may catch our spouse's eye, give each other a knowing nod of love, and then return to our conversations. There is a complicity that adds its pleasure, and often its spice, to the relationship.

When we are able to see our relationship, our marriage, as a place of safety and of freedom, we understand that marriage is two people living side by side, recognizing the innate worth of each other, and hence each other's independence. It is not two people trying to live as one, although early in our marriage, we were apt to think of ourselves as one, and we ran the risk of pursuing a sort of symbiosis. But with time, we learned that our relationship grew stronger when we allowed for space between us. Rainer Maria Rilke, in *Letters to a Young Poet*, writes that true love "consists in this, that two solitudes protect and border and salute each other."

Pierre and I return often to these words of Rilke as we try to give each other space for solitude. Even when we are home together, we try to find a place where one of us can close the door. We respect this space and if need be, we knock quietly on the door. These moments of solitude feed our spiritual being. We need them. Our relationship needs them. Likewise, we each sometimes go for a long walk alone. As much as we enjoy walking together and sharing our thoughts, there is also solace in walking alone and sharing our thoughts with ourselves.

When I do this, the trees are my company, and I am more apt to hug one as I know only the other trees are watching me.

Room for solitude and room for silence. Spaces of stillness dispersed throughout the day. We may sit quietly together outside, enjoying the fresh air, the sunshine, and the shade in summertime, the trees that surround our small backyard, the forsythia bush in the spring, the red and pink begonias in the summer. We do not need to talk. Or we may go for a walk together—feeling the ground underneath our feet, looking at the path ahead, the wildflowers on either side—without words. Or we may do a chore together, raking leaves, a whole backyard full, respecting each other's silent thoughts. Reading quietly, long into the night, downstairs on the couch, upstairs in bed side by side. Shared silence becomes communion and deepens our togetherness.

Such communion is built on respect, trust, and forgiveness. When Pierre and I spend time together in silence, we experience an underlying oneness that brings us close to all of humanity. This gives a new depth to our lives and points to our true purpose, to our true place on this earth. Two solitudes living in harmony with each other and with the world around them.

Seeing marriage as a sanctuary, a place of safety and freedom, expresses the wellbeing of our relationship. A wellbeing that is fed by springs of respect, trust, and forgiveness. A sense of wellbeing that I discovered as a child, close to my childhood pond, in the middle of the reeds and willow trees.

JOURNAL PRACTICE 20:
SILENCE AND SOLITUDE

Look back for a memory of silence, of solitude.

- How old were you?

- Did the experience surprise you?

- How long did it last?

- Where were you?

- Did it change anything?

- Did you talk about it with your spouse or partner?

- Have you thought about taking him or her there?

With each new journal entry, Thomas Merton felt he penetrated deeper into what he was living. Often he included his dreams. They were part of his life experience. In the last collection of his journal entries, The Other Side of the Mountain, *he wrote about a dream of November 19, 1968, three weeks before his untimely death. He was in the Himalayas. "I was looking at the mountain and it was pure white... and I heard a voice saying, 'There is another side of the mountain.'" He realized that every mountain has another side, the side that has never been photographed.*

🐚 SUGGESTION

Consider including dreams in your journal entries. Dreams open the door to your unconscious. They point the way to deeper living. So often—almost always—dreams disappear if we do not write them down. Try keeping a paper and pencil near your bed. Turn to it upon first awakening. Write your dream almost with your eyes closed. Don't think about it. Just remember it. Then in the morning copy it into your journal entry. Write a few lines about what the dream might be pointing to. Your journal writing will bridge the visible world and the invisible.

After a few minutes of silence, write a short journal entry about experiencing a moment of solitude, of peace. Maybe include part of a dream. Where does your journal writing lead you?

Share the moment with your partner. Think ahead to how you can look for more moments of solitude in your togetherness.

Put together these last three pages, "Memories of Wellbeing," as you continue to write your love story.

Acorn   *Giant Oak*

CHAPTER SEVEN

Celebrating: From Acorn to Giant Oak

Geneva, October 22

And now to celebrate. To celebrate how wonderful it is to wake up each morning in the arms of the man I have loved for more than fifty-five years.

Last night Pierre made us a cheese fondue—his recipe, with half Swiss Gruyère, half French Comté and bubbly white wine, making it a fondue royal. I lit lots of candles around our place settings—beige table cloth, white plates, beige napkins—and turned off the overhead light. I put on our favorite Paganini record. All was ready.

We were celebrating this last chapter of SIDE BY SIDE. *The book is Pierre's almost as well as mine. From its beginnings five years ago—when I wrote in my journal that I wanted to write about our lasting love—he has shared in the remembering. We have lived anew the good times and also the less good ones. It is our love story.*

Before sitting down, we danced to our favorite record—a slow tango. I asked him to remember with me the last time we tangoed. It was at our double eightieth birthday celebration. A grandson had found the music. It wasn't Paganini; instead it was a true tango. All our children and grandchildren surrounded us. I followed as Pierre led me through to the end. We were still young and beautiful.

This morning as Pierre cleaned the fondue pot and I served our breakfast coffee, I again realized how grateful I am—for our love, our family, our home. For the pleasant grounds where we live, the trees outside our kitchen window. The maple trees are holding on to the last of their bright red leaves.

The giant oak trees are still mostly green, with splashes of orange. Some of the rust-colored leaves are falling, along with some of the acorns. I will pick up a few of them this afternoon and start a new collection for our youngest grandchildren.

In the pages ahead, I have written about acorns, how they settle into the ground and wait for their shells to break, freeing the seed within. I let the acorn lead me to memories of celebration. From small celebrations, everyday ones, like our breakfast this morning, to big celebrations, like our double eightieth birthdays. From the small acorn to the giant oak tree.

From a short journal entry five years ago to a whole book today. A book celebrating our love. A book that I want to share so that other couples, young and old, may be led to celebrate lasting love.

EVERYDAY CELEBRATIONS

WHEN CELEBRATED, THE RELATIONSHIP BECOMES A source of daily delight. I return to Rumi's beautiful quote that I used in the first chapter, "Let the beauty we love be what we do. There are one hundred ways to kneel and kiss the ground." So, too, there are one hundred ways to celebrate our love.

To celebrate means to honor, to toast. We lift our wine glasses and toast to lasting love. There are special celebrations, special occasions. But there are also everyday celebrations. Loving someone is every day.

An oak tree is a celebration. It grew from the small acorn. The shell split open to free the seed. The stem within the seed grew a root at one end that found its way into the ground. At the other end, the stem grew a bud that grew into the trunk. The trunk put out branches, the branches put out leaves and acorns, the acorns put out seeds. And the story began anew. Each giant oak tree started from one small acorn. When we celebrate the giant oak tree, we are celebrating the achievement of the small acorn.

A loving couple is a celebration. From the acorn, from the small beginning of our relationship—the first awareness of the other, the first touch of Pierre's hand—we continue to discover one another and grow in love. Ideally, as I have suggested in this book, we make courtship a daily pleasure. Still today when Pierre and I take time to say I love you, there is celebration. There is no age in courtship. Just as there is no age in our commitment to living together, to making the commitment freely, to living it well. We look outward for fresh air and renewal, and inward for steadfastness and trust. We welcome new growth and strive for balance. We enjoy a sense of wellbeing and the comfort in knowing that we are appreciated. And we celebrate our love every day.

I wish it were that easy, but it is not. These continuing components are steps—steps that overlap, steps that come together, steps that are never finished—along the path of lasting love. And with each step, there is celebration. Celebrating both the tree and the acorn reminds us to celebrate our whole shared life. On a monthly date, we ask ourselves what we are doing to encourage the small acorn that began with our commitment to grow and to reach tall through branches to more leaves. What are we doing to celebrate our love?

How do we find these everyday moments of celebration? We open our eyes to them. They are all around us. Our breakfasts, sitting at the kitchen table, looking out at the maple trees, the oak trees. Seeing the daily Swiss flight arrive each morning from New York, a little after nine o'clock. We look up and say, Welcome! When our Brooklyn grandchildren were younger and flying in to see us, we would tell them to sit on the left side of the plane and remember to wave to us just before landing.

We find these happy moments in the way we look at each other. We look at what we like about the other's physical appearance. I like Pierre's deep-set eyes and thick eyebrows. I like his hands, the fifty-five-year-old wedding band. I like his broad back. I still see him tall, strong, and attractive. When he comes into my study, he is good-looking, engaging, appealing. I stand up to give him a kiss. A moment's hug.

We look also at what we appreciate about the other's temperament. When the other is relaxed—forehead without a frown, shoulders at ease, hands open. When the other is smiling. A smile is important and lightens the atmosphere. Pierre and I remind each other to smile more often. We see in photos how much more pleasant we look when we are smiling. And to laugh more often. When we laugh together, our laughter makes us feel good, it warms our dispositions. And it is contagious. When one of us laughs, the other joins in. If others are around, they will share in our laughter. We need to take the time to appreciate such moments. To tell our partner that they're really quite wonderful, that we like their good humor, their happy temperament, their quiet optimism. That we are grateful to be together. It's reason to celebrate.

Pierre and I have learned that the more we appreciate the other, the more loveable the other becomes. The more I appreciate when he pays attention to me, and the more I express my appreciation, the more attentive he becomes. Likewise, the more he appreciates when I am mild-mannered, the more mild-mannered I try to become. If I tell him that I feel loved when he takes time to listen, when he pays a compliment, he will more readily do so. Likewise, if he tells me he feels more loved when I kiss him more often, then I will more readily do so.

There are also everyday moments of looking together at something we both like. Looking at something inside the home. Stopping to look at the candles that light the dining room table. Appreciating their gentle glow on the silver place settings as we sit down to dinner. A moment to celebrate. Or looking at a painting that we love, remembering where it came from. Pierre and I have a favorite painting that we found at an outdoor market in southern France. The painting is of a couple sitting at a table in a café, it looks rather Chagall-like, with a crooked window and a bird in the background. It's unsigned. We say it's our Chagall. We enjoy looking at it together, there on the wall of our living room and remembering where we found it, how delighted we were to discover it. We could be the couple in the café that Chagall painted.

Likewise we enjoy looking at the pottery we have brought back from the monastery in the mountains above Geneva. Seeing each morning our breakfast coffee mugs, the ones *les petites soeurs*, the little sisters, make. The mugs are earthenware, a deep grey, warm and smooth to hold. They are made with love. It's like holding a prayer in our hands. We remember the quiet times on top of the mountain. We take time to relive these memories.

We are thankful for this everyday beauty in our home, the objects we have collected over the years, the gifts our children and friends have given us. The Navajo storyteller doll that we carefully picked out in Santa Fe, with the six children nestling in the mother's arms, listening to her stories. The smoky blue glass vase from Afghanistan that a U.N. peacekeeper gave us. It's placed on the oak cupboard in our front hall and greets us every time when we come home. All things to look at, to appreciate in our daily lives. Little everyday celebrations.

There's also looking at something we both appreciate outside the home. Come spring we admire the forsythia bush in our backyard and watch it slowly start to flower. We see the small buds bursting into bright yellow, then the whole branch blossoming, catching fire. Pierre puts out birdseed, and we love watching the sparrows arrive at the birdfeeder close by—how they flitter around it and then make room for one another. There is so much to look at around us—all the maple and oak trees and the lake constantly changing color. In the evening we'll go for a short walk to enjoy a sunset. We watch the sky turning pink, the clouds disappearing as the pink turns crimson. Later, we sometimes return outdoors, to take a few minutes to look up at the dark sky, to identify the Big Dipper, or to see that single star that the poet Rilke said was waiting for us to notice it.

We practice *seeing*, looking closely at something. "It doesn't have to be the blue iris, it could be weeds in a vacant lot… just pay attention," writes the poet Mary Oliver. To pay attention to what is around us when we're sitting in the backyard, when we go for a walk. And when we travel together, when we go to Paris on the TGV train to see our two children and their families. Instead of reading our newspapers and books the entire journey, we look at the rolling green countryside as we pass through Burgundy, the prosperous farms, the small villages with their red roofs.

Likewise, when we are in the States, on the Amtrak train from New York City to Boston. We sit on the side of the train close to the ocean and wait for the colorful village of Mystic, remembering the many happy summers when we stayed with friends in the small village of Noank close by, looking at the boats sail by to the harbor.

Everyday moments that call out to us, telling us to slow down, to take time to see the beauty around us. And to celebrate our togetherness.

JOURNAL PRACTICE 21:
EVERYDAY MOMENTS OF CELEBRATION

Find a memory of an everyday moment when you and your partner saw something that brought you pleasure, that made you both feel good.

- Were you outside?

- In a new place?

- Or a place you return to often?

- Was there bright daylight?

- What did you say?

- What did you feel?

- Did you reach out to your partner?

- Was there a desire to draw close together?

In this chapter, I return to Rainer Maria Rilke, our mentor in the first chapter. This time to his book, Letters on Cezanne, *letters written to his wife, Clara, while he was living in Paris. "September 13, 1913, Never have I been so touched by the sight of heather as the other day when I found these three branches in your dear letter." He describes the branches, how they look like an embroidery, like three cypresses woven into a Persian rug with violet silk. He remembers when he walked back home in an abundance of heather. He is writing a love letter, wanting to share his joy in looking at her gift of three branches of heather.*

🌼 SUGGESTION

A journal entry can be very similar to a love letter. Addressing an entry to someone you love gives it an intimacy that brings warmth to your words. Rilke was writing each day to his wife, sharing his thoughts about Cezanne's painting. The subject of his letters, the paintings, glowed with his love for Clara. In writing your journal entry as if you were writing a letter to a friend, it takes on a personal tone. The subject of the entry glows with friendship.

Write your journal entry as if you are addressing your partner. Imagine your partner listening to you.

Then read your page together. It is a page composed for your partner. Enjoy being the two of you.

MOMENTS OF LISTENING,
TOUCHING, SMELLING, TASTING

ALONG WITH MOMENTS OF SEEING, THERE ARE MOMENTS of listening. When one of us hears birdsong, we can call the other to listen. Birds sing every day, we can listen every day. When the birds wake early in the morning, we, too, can wake and greet the day together. We have friends who recognize the different birdsongs, who go on bird walks together. For now, we are just reminding ourselves to listen, to wake up and listen together to the birds as they greet the morning light. I have read in Terry Tempest Williams recent memoir, *When Women Were Birds*, that birds do not always sing the same song at the same time of the day. "Each bird may sing differently from time to time." Pierre and I have lessons to learn together.

We listen to our favorite CDs, mostly classical—Mozart, Vivaldi, Boccherini—still discovering composers whom we are not familiar with. Sometimes we take out our old long-playing records. We stop what we are doing and listen together to Louis Armstrong and remember when a celebrated poet friend, Amy Clampitt, discovered the record in our cupboard and danced to it with her partner Hal. To be grateful for music. To be grateful for the piano, for the pleasure of playing a few measures of Bach or Beethoven and for the pleasure of listening. A familiar tune. In this Indian summer of our marriage, it's Pierre's turn to play. And when the children come, it's their turn. It is our joy to listen. And now we listen also to our grandchildren who are learning to play. A celebration of family continuity around the piano.

And voices on the phone, on Skype. When our youngest granddaughter calls and says, "Granddaddy..." Just her voice warms Pierre's heart. *"Comment vas-tu, Clementine?"* "How are you, Clementine?" And she responds in perfect French. *"Bien. Je suis en vacances."* "I'm fine. I'm on vacation." This little granddaughter who lives in Brooklyn speaks to him in both English and French. He will ask her what she is doing on vacation. Is she playing with her older brother or with her friend who lives upstairs? He will listen to her words, he will listen still more to the sound of her loveable voice.

Listening also to television, finding favorite programs, concerts, movies, documentaries. We have made a little ritual of watching an international news channel each evening before supper; first CNN International or BBC, followed by Euronews in French. It's our "happy hour," with a glass of wine, the two of us, every evening. Rituals are important in a relationship. We look forward to them and unconsciously draw strength from them. When such rituals become routines, it's time to find ways to enliven them or to choose other ones.

I think of another ritual, short and brilliant. When Pierre opens a bottle of champagne, just the noise of the cork popping makes us rejoice. The sound means celebration.

Touching. How can we celebrate our sense of touch? We can remember to not let a day go by without touching each other.

A kiss, a hand on the shoulder, a quick back rub. The caresses we give to each other as we rest in bed. There is the deeper act of lovemaking, feeling the warmth of the other's body, the slow arousal, sharing the heightened response. Giving pleasure, receiving pleasure. The hidden world of creative love when we celebrate our mutual gift to the other.

When we are sitting side by side or walking side by side, we reach out to let the other know we are close to them. Sometimes the touch of Pierre's fingers on my hand is amazingly sensual. This comes with a whole way of being. We are relaxed and comfortable with one another.

We also touch our children and we let ourselves be touched. I give my big warm hugs mostly to my three daughters, but maybe with age, or maybe simply catching up with the times, I find I am also hugging my three sons. A moment's embrace. And when my children put their hands on my back, affectionately, I want to hold the moment for a long time. Pierre is more reserved. The French are more reserved. They give kisses on the two cheeks. They do not hug. But with all of us embracing one another—children and grandchildren—he, too, is warming to the practice.

There are the senses of smell and taste. A favorite perfume. Pierre misses the scent of Shalimar when I forget to spray it on me as I get dressed. It has been my perfume since our marriage. When I try to change, he claims he does not recognize me. We share the joy of other smells—lilac blossoms in our backyard, the honeysuckle on the wall not far from our front door. Or when one of us picks a branch of rosemary, brings it to the kitchen, and together we enjoy its scent—reminding us of southern France, of when we lived there early in our marriage. There were huge bushes of wild rosemary everywhere. We would bring home armfuls from our walks. The kitchen would be full of the fragrance; so would be our arms.

Certain tastes are also celebrations. Deep red cherries. Putting them in our mouth, maybe two at a time, crushing them with our tongue, gently biting into them. Watching Pierre do the same, enjoying both his pleasure and my own. Or savoring mango sorbet, the tangy flavor, the smooth cool texture, holding a spoonful on our tongue. I watch Pierre do this. I watch him hold each spoonful in his mouth. As I remember these moments, even my writing becomes more sensual.

When the two sensations of smell and taste come together, it can be a love feast! Smelling and tasting. And I return to our favorite cheese fondue, Pierre's specialty, with a French recipe from Haute Savoie, where he grew up, claiming it is the best. We had a family contest last Christmas to choose between three different ways to make cheese fondue. Three fondues, made with different cheeses, different wines, by the father and two of his sons. There were close to twenty of us, standing up, circling the table, tasting the three different fondues. Then we voted. The Swiss fondue made by our piano-playing son who lives in Fribourg won, but I still prefer my husband's.

And maybe what I like most about cheese fondue is the nutmeg that we grind fresh onto our plates, filling the room with its aroma, that we dip the piece of bread and cheese into before eating it. Nutmeg is an aphrodisiac. We dip into it liberally. The word takes us to Aphrodite, The Greek goddess of love and beauty. Certain smells awaken us to physical love and let us celebrate each other's beauty.

Smelling and tasting. Remembering. Everyday celebrations that awaken our senses. That let us learn anew to see, listen, touch, smell, and taste. To appreciate these moments together. To see the single star, to listen to the birds at dawn, to touch our partner's hand, to smell fresh rosemary, to taste the mango sherbet. To grow in love, the way the acorn grows to be the oak tree. All different ways to be thankful for another day of loving.

JOURNAL PRACTICE 22:
MOMENTS OF LISTENING,
TOUCHING, TASTING

Choose an experience involving one of the senses, something that you and your partner enjoyed together. Perhaps the sense of taste.

- Was it a first-time experience?
- If not, what was special this time?
- How did it awaken the sense of taste?
- Did the pleasure last?
- Did it awaken the same feeling for both of you?
- Did you look to repeat the pleasure?

In Letters on Cezanne, *Rilke writes about the branches of heather that his wife Clara enclosed in her letter, "their strong and serious smell, which is really just the fragrance of autumn earth." It is a fragrance, he writes, "that is bitter when it borders on taste." Rilke is celebrating the heather, finding the words to let Clara share the experience. Speaking of the earthy smell of the heather. Of autumn earth. He is not composing formal prose, but rather writing conversational prose, a letter.*

❧ SUGGESTION

Journal writing is conversational prose. It can be expressive, you can listen to your sentences. You can hear the repetition of certain sounds, the S in "strong and serious smell." You can see and smell the autumn earth. The sounds and images come from memory. And they come with practice. In writing a journal entry, you do not consciously try to compose sentences full of sounds and images. You let your hand and heart lead you. However the more you write, the more expressive your journal becomes.

Describe the memory in a very short journal entry. Give yourself time to read it and to see if it is expressive. Read it aloud. Let your words flow.

Read aloud your page to your spouse or partner. See if your words summon the same pleasure for your partner.

SPECIAL CELEBRATIONS

THERE ARE ALSO SPECIAL OCCASIONS OF CELEBRATION. Special events, special occurrences. Birthdays and anniversaries. What do we do to make each other's birthday special? To welcome them as opportunities to do something out of the ordinary? I ask myself, what does Pierre especially like? Not something I think he likes, or something I think he should like. And perhaps not something material. Rather, what does he enjoy? Come his next birthday, I will try to surprise Pierre. Maybe I will take him on a favorite walk in the Jura Mountains, where we often went with the children and picnicked—in the spring, in May, the month of his birthday, when there were little wild jonquils everywhere. We will see if they are still there.

Likewise, we can look together for original ways to celebrate our children's birthdays. This has become difficult for Pierre and me with our large family and now all the lively grandkids. But every now and then, we can try to think of something different. Instead of a gift, maybe some activity to do with them—an afternoon at the circus, a chairlift up to the top of a mountain. When a granddaughter recently turned twenty, I asked her what she would like for a special dinner. She surprised me and said American meatloaf. I suggested she come and make it with me. Together our four hands mixed the meat and onions and parsley and then shaped the large loaf.

I remember a surprise party I planned for Pierre's thirtieth birthday. We were living in Brussels, and I was expecting our number three on close to the same day. I took to bed, saying that the contractions were stronger and stronger. Pierre left to get the babysitter, as planned. In his absence, a dozen or more friends arrived and hid in the closets, behind the curtains, under the tables. Our two children got into bed with me. Pierre returned out of breath. He called and came to the bedroom door. "Surprise!" everyone shouted. Number three was born three days later.

We can continue to look for unique ways to celebrate. Quieter ones perhaps. Dinner parties, dances, dressing up, delighting in each other's company. All special occasions to celebrate. We look at our calendars. Is there something fun to look forward to? Such occasions give anticipation to the relationship. They add flavor, keep it from becoming dull, monotonous. To plan ahead, maybe something special each month, to celebrate togetherness.

There are special moments on vacations as we discover new places or return to places we know and want to appreciate again. When we are able to take a vacation, no matter how long or short, we discover the sights, sounds, smells, and tastes of a place all in one go. We open our arms to each other. For many years, when the children were young, our annual "honeymoon," our weekend away, was close by on the Lac d'Annecy. Friends would take care of our children, and another weekend we would take care of their children. We had a favorite restaurant, with tables close to the water. We would go there on Friday evening, all our senses alive for a weekend of love—our table reserved, the smell of fresh fish grilled with fennel, the proximity of the lake, the small waves lapping against the wooden pier, the sky slowly growing dark above the blue lake.

And discovering new experiences. This summer Pierre and I took two of our grandchildren on a walk to a waterfall in the French Alps. We walked along a path through the woods. The waterfall was hidden and high above. Before seeing it, we heard it. Then it was there, right in front of us, cascading over the cliff. I climbed down over the rocks with my granddaughter and we took off our sneakers and socks to put our feet in the ice cold water. Pierre and his grandson climbed out farther on the rocks, the water swirling round them, the mist spraying their faces. Together the four of us celebrated the power and the majesty of the waterfall.

Then there is the celebration that I have mentioned of our double eightieth birthdays. Although Pierre is a year and a few months older than I, we decided to celebrate them together so that our children and grandchildren wouldn't have to do it twice. We celebrated for the entire weekend, with the anniversary dinner at our favorite restaurant here in Bellevue on the lake. There were highlights every moment, I will name two. Our three daughters playing a Waltz for Six Hands by Rachmaninoff—the sight of their six hands gliding over the piano keys; I cried. All those years of piano lessons.

The second moment deserves an entire paragraph. Our middle daughter had found flying lanterns to celebrate our birthdays. She had a memory from long ago of the Montgolfier that her French grandfather once sent into the sky when we were living in Italy. She was only four years old. The very large paper balloon rose high into the sky, lifted by the heat from an alcohol lamp. Our daughter found smaller ones, a meter in height. At midnight—a complete surprise to the rest of us—she and her husband called us to the terrace. Each family had a white paper lantern. Together we lit small solid alcohol candles and waited for our lanterns to fill with hot air and lift into the night sky. They floated away, higher and higher. It was a clear night, filled with stars and flying lanterns. We were all ages, from the youngest grandchildren to Pierre and me, all making wishes, celebrating the love that holds us together.

To remember the acorn and the oak tree, its branches and its autumn leaves, all that has flourished from that first time we came together.

❧

I cannot make believe that all is perfect, closing my eyes to what goes wrong. And there will be things that continue to go wrong. One of us will feel unappreciated and taken for granted. We will grow angry with the other, turn our back, close the door. When this happens, we will try again to put the disagreement to the side until we are in a quieter mood, until we are ready to listen again to each other. Sometimes we have to wait a long time to say we are sorry. To say we will try to be more loving.

Learning to cope with disagreements, deceptions, disappointments. And learning also to cope with misfortune, accidents, ill health. We continue to need armfuls of good humor to remember when it was easier, the happier times, and armfuls of patience to wait for these better moments to return.

The acorn does not become an oak tree without the seasons, without rain, without sunshine. So it is for a relationship. It needs spring blossoms and autumn leaves. There is a natural rhythm in loving. We have seen it in each chapter. A rhythm to courtship as we grow older and we remember the hidden side of the nautilus shell, the side of lovemaking and stoking the fires in the alchemical furnace. To commitment, remembering the maple leaf in the dish on our kitchen table and realizing that the choice is ours each day, how to love the other and how to be loved.

A rhythm to looking both outward and inward. To look at the sunflowers, standing tall and leaving room for the other. And to look at the spark in the sea glass that glows after being tossed about in the sea. A rhythm to growing and staying green like the ivy, sometimes holding on, sometimes letting go. A rhythm to being well, green like my childhood pond.

And finally a rhythm to celebrating, moments of joy and moments of thanksgiving. From acorn to giant oak, from courtship to celebration. The unending and overlapping stages of love. To be grateful each morning for another day of loving. Grateful to be side by side.

JOURNAL PRACTICE 23:
SPECIAL MOMENTS OF CELEBRATION

For this last practice, write a short love letter to your partner.

- Make a list of what you appreciate about him or her.

- What do you appreciate the most?

- Has it always been so?

- Have you told your partner?

- Have you celebrated recently your love?

- What did you do?

- What would you hope for tomorrow?

In a letter from Letters on Cezanne, *dated October 13, Rilke writes, "Early this morning I read about your autumn, and all the colors you brought into your letter filled my mind with strength and radiance." Filled his mind with radiance. He saw his wife walking through the colors of autumn in their home in Germany, while he was in Paris, and he was admiring "its dissolving brightness." Although they were separated, through their letters, they are sharing—reliving—the brightness of autumn.*

🍀 SUGGESTION

Writing journal entries and letters by hand is very different than touching keys on a keyboard. First you allow yourself to slow down. To find a comfortable chair in a place that is conducive to personal writing. To choose a pen you like. To feel the paper. And to be present for the moment. Nothing is asking you to rush forward. Many writers feel it is easier this way to let their imaginations take over. Let your heart speak. See in your imagination the little acorn. Then the giant oak tree. Be confident and reach that high with your love.

Write a love letter. Give the place and date. Maybe list all that you love about your spouse or partner. And close with what you love most.

Find the right moment to give your love letter to your partner. Share the brightness.

Then gather all your pages together in a notebook. Look for a notebook that feels comfortable in your hands. Insert the pages or copy them, slowly, remembering and enjoying each memory. If you wish, include your love letter at the end.

This is your love story. Celebrate your togetherness!

Acknowledgments

First i thank my husband pierre for being at my side since we first fell in love in the azalea gardens of the Villa Carlotta, close to sixty years ago. I thank him for all the years of unending courtship and celebration, including the many steps in between.

And I thank him for being at my side as I wrote this book, for remembering together the good, and sometimes the less good, moments of our relationship, for listening and reading the numerous early drafts, and for encouraging me every day as we relived our love story.

I thank also our six children who continue to enrich our days and who teach us to keep growing. To reach for the stars together. With a boost from our wonderful fifteen grandchildren.

Then I thank my brilliant editor Melissa Rosati at Red Lotus Studio Press, who has made the book possible. A writer, an editor, a publisher, and, most important, a friend. Thank you, Melissa, for believing in this book. Melissa's publishing team made this book come alive on the printed page and in ebook formats. I thank Betsy Robinson for her insightful comments and editorial expertise. Sophie Kelle and Jason Leung, Infinitum Limited, are book design artists and digital content magicians.

I am grateful also to the generous readers who helped me along the way.

To my parents for their loving example, my sister for her encouragement. To my writing friends in the Geneva Writers' Group and the International Women's Writing Guild. And to all our friends with whom we continue to celebrate anniversaries of lasting love.

READING TOGETHER:
The Author's Top 10 List

THROUGHOUT *SIDE BY SIDE*, I'VE GIVEN EXAMPLES OF books that have influenced our life together. Recently, Pierre and I were asked to consider the top ten titles that brought us closer together. This was a powerful and fulfilling exercise. I hope you will do the same with your partner.

Seven Story Mountain, Thomas Merton. This is the book we shared through letter writing during the year after falling in love. And then was followed some years later by *New Seeds of Contemplation*, where Merton moves from the traditional Catholic writer to the universal spiritual writer.

An Interrupted Life and Letters from Westerbork, Etty Hillesum. An extraordinary book written in journals that gave Pierre and me reason to hold on to hope, and faith and love.

The Prophet, Kahil Gilbran. We have returned to this book often, with wisdom about love, marriage, children, joy and sorrow, good and evil, beauty...and more.

The Alchemist, Paulo Coelho. His writing made us open our hearts to our dreams.

Siddhartha, Hermann Hesse. This inviting book helps us to better understand our own spiritual path.

Memories, Dreams, Reflections, C. G. Jung. Pierre has not read this from the first page to the last, but we have read together for close to thirty years many portions, assimilating together a little, little bit of Jung's genius.

Dreams from my Father, Barack Obama. A book we loved, giving us a deeper appreciation of Obama, of his inheritance.

The Testament of Mary, Colm Toibin. A moving novel, one that invites us re-imagine the origins of our Christian faith.

Mirrors, Stories of Almost Everyone, Eduardo Galleano. For the last few years, often at lunch, we read one of these fragments covering the history of our world, thought provoking always.

The Invention of Wings, Sue Monk Kidd. This book made us still more aware of the destructive seeds of racism and the courage of those opposing it, from the Grimké sisters up to Martin Luther King.

Bibliography

Basho, Matsuo, *The Narrow Road to the Deep North* (London: Penguin Books, 1966)

Brande, Dorothea, *Becoming a Writer* (New York: Harcourt Brace & Company, 1934)

Dillard, Annie, *The Writing Life* (New York: Harper & Row, 1989)
For the Time Being (New York: Knopf, 1999)

Eckhart, Meister, *Selected Writings* (London: Penguin Classic, 1994)

Jung, Carl G., *Memories, Dreams, Reflections* (London: Fontana Paperbacks, 1969)
The Undiscovered Self (Canada: Little, Brown & Company, 1957)
The Portable Jung, edited by Joseph Campbell (New York: Penguin Books, 1976)

Gibran, Kahlil, *The Prophet* (New York: Alfred A. Knopf, 1953)

Hamilton, Edith, *Mythology*, Baucis and Philemon (New York: New American Library, 1969)

Hildegard of Bingen, *Illuminations of Hildegard of Bingen* (Santa Fe: Bear & Company, 1985)

Hillesum, Etty, *An Interrupted Life* (New York: Henry Holt, 1986)

Merton, Thomas, *The Seven Storey Mountain* (New York: Harcourt Brace & Company, 1948)
Zen and the Birds of Appetite (New York: New Directions, 1968)
The Other Side of the Mountain, The Journals of Thomas Merton, Volume Seven, 1967-68 (New York: Harper Collins, 1999)

Nhat Hanh, Thich, *Peace Is Every Step* (New York: Bantam Books, 1992)

Obama, Barack, *Dreams from My Father* (New York: Three Rivers Press, 1995)

Oliver, Mary, *Thirst* (Boston, Beacon Press, 2007).

Rilke, Rainer Maria, *Letters to a Young Poet* (New York: Norton, 1963)
Letters on Cézanne (New York: Farrar, Straus and Giroux, 2002)
Duino Elegies (Einsiedeln, Switzerland: Daimon Verlag 1992)

Rumi, Jelaluddin, *The Essential Rumi*, translated by Coleman Barks (New York: Harper Collins, 1995)

Teilhard de Chardin, Pierre, *Hymn of the Universe* (New York: Harper & Row, 1961)

Tiberghien, Susan, *Looking for Gold* (Einsiedeln, Switzerland: Daimon Verlag, 1997)
Circling to the Center (New York: Paulist Press, 2000)

Ueland, Brenda, *If you Want to Write* (St. Paul, MN: Graywolf, 1987)

Williams, Terry Tempest, *When Women Were Birds* (Farrar, Straus and Giroux, 2012)

Zinsser, William, *On Writing Well* (New York: Harper Perennial, 1990)
Inventing the Truth (Boston: Houghton Mifflin, 1995)

Susan M. Tiberghien

About the Author

Susan M. Tiberghien is the author of three memoirs and the bestselling nonfiction book, *One Year to a Writing Life*. Her first book, *Looking for Gold: A Year in Jungian Analysis*, was published when she turned sixty. This is a lesson she happily shares: there is time!

Side by Side: Writing Your Love Story is the book closest to her heart because it shares her love for a Frenchman and her love for writing. Tiberghien has taught creative writing for over twenty-five years at writers' centers and conferences across the States and Europe, at C. G. Jung Societies, for the International Women's Writing Guild, and each month for the Geneva Writers' Group that she founded twenty years ago.

She lives in Geneva with her French husband. Some of her six children live close by, the others live in Paris and in Brooklyn.

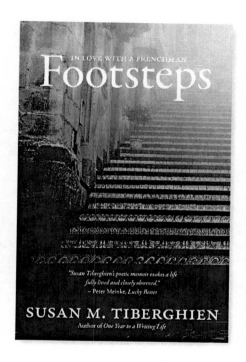

Pierre-Yves and Susan Tiberghien

CPSIA information can be obtained at www.ICGtesting.com
Printed in the USA
LVOW08s1140111015

457798LV00006B/678/P